The WEEKENDER'S GARDENING M·A·N·U·A·L

Easy-Care Gardens in Two Hours (or Less!) a Week

PATRICIA A. TAYLOR

An Owl Book
HENRY HOLT AND COMPANY
NEW YORK

A FRIEDMAN GROUP BOOK

Henry Holt and Company, Inc.
Publishers since 1866
115 West 18th Street
New York, New York 10011

Henry Holt® is a registered
trademark of Henry Holt and Company, Inc.

Library of Congress Cataloging-in-Publication Data
Taylor, Patricia A., 1938–
The weekender's gardening manual.
Includes index.
1. Gardening. I. Title.
SB453T2859 1986 635 85-21856

ISBN 0-8050-1024-6 (An Owl book: pbk.)

Henry Holt books are available for special promotions
and premiums. For details contact: Director, Special Markets.

First published in hardcover in 1986 by
Holt, Rinehart and Winston.

First Owl Book Edition—1989

THE WEEKENDER'S GARDENING MANUAL:
Easy-Care Gardens in Two Hours (or Less!) a Week
was prepared and produced by
Michael Friedman Publishing Group, Inc.
15 West 26th Street
New York, NY 10010

Editor: Karla Olson
Art Director and Designer: Richard Boddy
Photo Researcher: Susan M. Duane
Production Manager: Karen L. Greenberg
Illustrations by Grace Tvaryanas

Typeset by BPE Graphics, Inc.
Printed and bound in China by Leefung-Asco Printers Ltd.

3 5 7 9 10 8 6 4 2

For my family: Toby, Katherine, Anne

ACKNOWLEDGMENTS

Gardeners love to show off their creations and to share their wealth of experience. Over the years, my garden has come into being through the contributions of plants and advice from many friends, particularly Olivet Beckwith, Edith Bowman, Isabelle Braunlich, Lisa Corey, Mary Gibbs, Lee Haines, Dorothy O'Neill, Florence Phillips, Corinne Rowley, Eleanor B. Taylor, and Jean Woodward. Much of the information they have given me is contained in this book.

Other gardeners have good libraries to back up their statements. Two—Joyce Boyle and Sarah Lewis—were particularly kind in providing me with out-of-print research material from their collections.

Though not one other member of my family is a gardener, all helped with the book in their own way. My husband, Toby, read all drafts to make sure the material would be intelligible to a novice; my eleven-year-old daughter, Katherine, worked with me in proofing all the botanical names and verifying the hardiness and availability of all plants listed in Appendix A; and my seven-year-old daughter, Anne, gave me hugs for encouragement and a handmade congratulations card on the day I sent the manuscript to the publisher.

It is thus with great pleasure that I acknowledge the friendship and family affection that form the true foundation for this book. May all gardeners be so blessed.

C O N T E N T S

PREFACE

A weekend gardener is a special kind of person, one who is in contact with the garden only from Friday evening through Sunday evening. This is a commuter who treks long hours from a suburban home to a city job or a city resident who flees a hectic pace for a relaxing sojourn at a weekend country retreat. Time is a precious commodity for such a person; a garden can be allotted no more than two hours on the weekend.

If you would like to have a garden and the description above describes your life-style, then this is the book for you. It assumes that you are a relative newcomer to gardening and that you don't want to spend the time to become an expert. You really are not interested in learning all the nitty-gritty about every leaf and petal. All you want are some pretty flowers and perhaps some fresh vegetables.

USING THIS BOOK
HOW IT IS ORGANIZED

This book is designed to give you as much free time as possible. As such, it is relatively long on illustration and short on words. Flip through the pages and see if a flower illustration, garden scheme, or planting technique captures your eye. If it does, read the accompanying text.

If you feel quite serious about your weekend garden, read Chapter Two. It describes what is expected of you during the garden seasons of the year and includes basic information such as ordering from catalogs, preparing the soil, planting seedlings, controlling weeds, and cleaning up the garden. The next three sections—Chapters Three, Four, and Five—give specific examples of garden designs. These are all easy to maintain and you should find some helpful ideas for your weekend garden. Chapter Six stresses the importance of establishing a good relationship with your local nursery and reviews some of the steps you can take to combat insects and diseases. Chapter Seven consists of a small pep talk that tells you to stop reading and to start digging—and to have fun in the process.

The appendixes are designed to serve as your basic reference guide; they are crucial to the book. Indeed, this book differs from many other garden guides in that all plants listed in the garden plans and in the text are described in detail in the appendixes. These appendixes contain three listings of plants: those you should definitely consider (Appendix A), those you might want to take a chance on (Appendix B), and those you should avoid (Appendix C). All plants that are included in Appendix A can be grown in areas where the temperatures fall as low as minus twenty degrees (minus twenty-nine degrees Celsius). This feature saves you the trouble of having to look up the hardiness zone for any plant in this section.

This book not only recommends plants to grow in your weekend garden, it also tells you how to get them. All plants in Appendix A can be obtained from at least one of five mail-order nurseries mentioned in the section's introduction. In addition, Appendix D gives the names and addresses of all members of the Mail Order Association of Nurserymen.

So there you are: gorgeous pictures to inspire you, practical tips to guide you, and detailed information to help you. Being a weekend gardener will be a cinch. Go to it!

CHAPTER ONE

THE WEEKEND GARDEN

What kind of a garden can you have with only two hours of care each week? Quite a nice one, as a matter-of-fact. First, however, you must decide on the kind of garden you want. *Garden,* by the way, is defined in this book as a plot of land where herbs, vegetables, or flowers are grown. (*Webster's Dictionary, Seventh Edition,* uses similar terminology in its primary definition of the word.) Trees, shrubs, bushes, and lawns are not included; they are assumed to be part of the landscape, which is quite different from the garden.

SETTING YOUR OBJECTIVES
FOUR KEY QUESTIONS YOU MUST ANSWER

Even by narrowing the definition of garden to exclude trees and shrubs, you are still presented with a tremendous range of plants to grow. Answer the following questions to help you narrow down your list.

QUESTION ONE. *Why do you want a garden?* There are three answers to consider here: for viewing pleasure, for harvesting (in the form of cut flowers or vegetables), or for a combination of viewing and harvesting.

If you want a garden for viewing pleasure, you can have lovely designs using ground covers, decorative plants such as hostas, or pretty annuals such as begonias. These are

Decorative gardens are designed to be looked at but not touched; they supply no cuttings for arrangements. Easy to maintain, decorative gardens are often found in shaded areas.

plants that will look attractive in your yard and require a minimum amount of work. Gardeners who must contend with deep shade often have to settle for this kind of garden.

Or you may decide that indoor flower arrangements or vegetable dishes are more important to you than the design of the garden outdoors. Plants that mainly serve decorative purposes in the garden are not for you.

If you are the kind of gardener who not only likes to admire the garden but also likes to harvest some of its bounty in the form of cut flowers or vegetables for the table, you want the most utilitarian kind of garden. It means a bit more work, but also more pleasure. Except for the deep shade garden, all designs in this book are in this category.

QUESTION TWO. *Where do you want your garden?* To some degree, the answer to this question depends on why you want a garden. If you want a garden for viewing pleasure, for example, you will want it prominently displayed so that you and your friends and family can enjoy it constantly. A cutting garden, on the other hand, is often tucked away in a corner so that its depredations are not noticed.

The site you choose for your garden will often affect its size. For example, if you want to put a garden between the walk to your front door and the house itself, you are limited to the distance between the walk and the house. On the other hand, if you have a large yard, you could put a garden

Cut-flower gardens consist of plants to be snipped without mercy. Often these gardens are tucked away in seldom-viewed corners so deprivation from cutting will not be noticed.

wherever you please. It is best, however, to start off small in your first year or two of gardening and then to expand with experience. There is, however, no reason why you can't have a weekend garden that borders an area 125 feet (thirty-eight meters) long; this kind of garden is illustrated in Chapter Four.

The garden site is also a factor in the decision of whether to have a formal or informal garden. A formal garden is one with a definite floral pattern; indeed, the pattern rather than the flowers themselves often determines the attraction of the garden. You need a geometrically shaped flower bed, such as a circle or a square, to construct such a garden. An informal garden can fit into any garden space. This kind of garden need not be without its own internal design mechanism, but it is one without an overall rigid pattern. Both kinds of gardens are attractive; each requires very different kinds of implementation. Your first step is to decide which kind you want.

Once you've chosen your site, take a look at the amount of sun that shines on the intended garden spot. Sun will be a key factor in determining what plants you will grow. If, for example, you've chosen a cozy, shady nook nestled under some maple trees, you can forget any plans for growing colorful annuals such as marigolds, zinnias, and petunias. These are all sun-lovers and will simply fade away in the

A utilitarian garden is appreciated for both its beauty and its potential harvest of cut flowers or fresh vegetables. This kind of garden requires more work in terms of design scheme, harvest schedule, and weekly maintenance. When reaping the bounty of a lovely garden, however, the extra effort seems worth it.

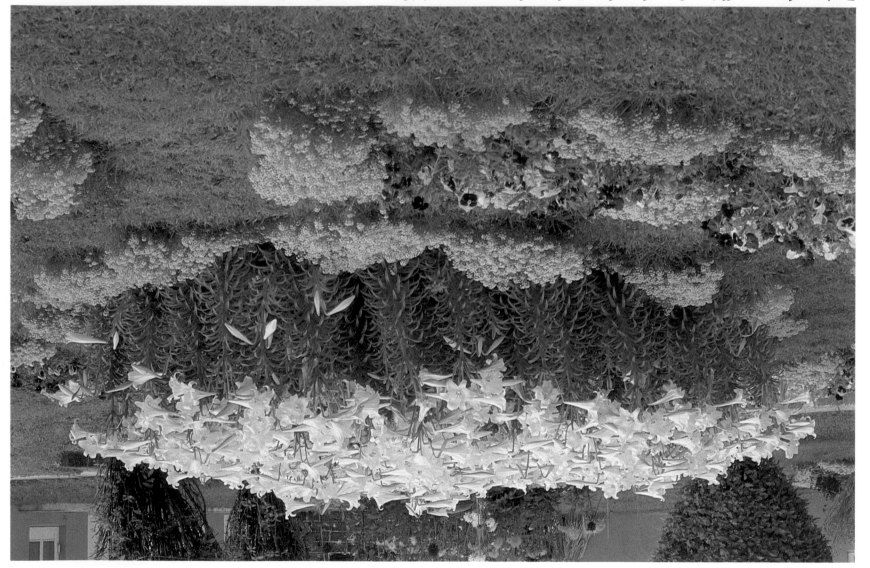

Design rules over all in a formal garden. Such gardens are very rigid in structure but always create a pleasing effect.

An informal garden often gives the illusion of wandering at will, but in reality it has an interior design pattern.

Sun gardens, the most intensely colored of all, add a bright spot to summer landscapes. Marigolds are often a featured performer.

Shade gardens are more subdued in appearance. The cool, elegant leaves of the hosta plant are a staple in these kinds of gardens.

shade. In this aspect, the answer for Question Two is closely tied to that for Question Three.

QUESTION THREE. *What do you want in the garden?*
Up until this point, the text has mentioned both vegetables and flowers. Do you want both or just one of these kinds of plants? You must have at least six full hours of sun a day to grow vegetables. There are flowers, however, that will grow in any kind of garden light. Although it is possible to incorporate vegetables into the flower garden, and vice versa, this book treats each separately. There are two chapters on flower gardens and one on a vegetable garden.

If you have decided on flowers, you must then ask if you want perennials, biennials, annuals, or a combination of all three. For the purposes of this book, *perennial* is defined as a plant that blooms every year and whose roots winter over; *biennial* as a plant that bears foliage one year, flowers the next, and then dies; and *annual* as a plant that blooms for one year and whose roots then die; many annuals reseed themselves, however, and have descendants that appear the next year. Each kind of flower has advantages and disadvantages. Perennials usually come back every year, which saves you lots of planting time. However, most perennials tend to have restricted flowering periods; once they are

Perennial gardens are a special delight because their flowers come back every year—much like good friends stopping by for a regular visit. Many perennials only bloom for a short time, however; this presents a drawback for some and a challenge for others. Those who do grow perennials are rewarded with a changing variety of color and form.

through blooming, you have either a bare or a plain green spot in your garden. Annuals, on the other hand, usually bloom all summer long and are a constant source of color in the garden. Some people view this as a drawback, however, because it means the garden remains the same all summer long and never changes color.

QUESTION FOUR. *When do you want a garden?* This book assumes that all the gardens will experience temperatures below freezing during the winter months. With such climate variations, there are definite seasons for different plants. Are you at your weekend residence every weekend, or are there times when you are away for an extended period? If, for example, you are gone during the summer, it makes no sense to plant perennials that bloom at that time. Perhaps you only visit occasionally during the spring—why then bother putting in a lot of daffodils?

Once you decide on which seasons you want your garden to be in bloom, it is important to realize that each season has different planting and maintenance requirements. Watering, for example, is rarely a problem in spring but is usually a weekly chore during the drier summer months. All the gardens illustrated in this book cover three seasons; you may wish to eliminate some recommendations because you will not be physically present to enjoy them.

Annual gardens are filled with color. Since they are planted anew each year, you can easily change design and color schemes. With a minimum amount of care, most annuals will be covered with blossoms all summer long and supply a constant source of cut flowers for indoor arrangements.

Spring gardens, with their easy-to-maintain bulbs, provide colorful news that dreary winter has ended.

Summer gardens generally reflect the brilliance of the sun. Watering is usually a weekly chore during this time of year.

RECOGNIZING THE LIMITATIONS

YOU WILL NOT BE ABLE TO GROW EVERYTHING

Now that you've answered the who, what, when, where, and why questions, this book will tell you how to go about implementing your decisions. A word of caution is in order, however. It really is easy and possible to be a weekend gardener and to enjoy the results, but be aware of the limitations. There are three particularly important ones.

LIMITATION ONE. *For the most part, you will have to buy seedlings in containers rather than seeds.* The latter need too much watering and thinning after germination for the weekend gardener. You will find that not all plants are available as seedlings or as root stocks and that it is more expensive to start a garden this way. On the other hand, it is also a lot easier.

LIMITATION TWO. *You will have to avoid plants that need extra care and attention.* Examples of such plants are given in Appendix C. Tall, elegant plants, such as delphiniums and hollyhocks, are included in this category. While it is a shame to go without them, they simply require time that the weekend gardener does not have. A good rule of thumb for a beginning weekend gardener is to avoid all plants more than three feet (one meter) tall.

Chrysanthemum-filled fall gardens are treasured because they present a last touch of color before the onset of winter.

LIMITATION THREE. *It's a waste of time and effort to have plants with short bloom periods.* Remember, you really will be enjoying your garden only two out of seven days. You could entirely miss a plant that bears flowers for no more than four or five days; or you might get to see the flowers for only one weekend. The flowers of the gladiolus, are an example that falls into this category.

REVIEWING OTHER ASPECTS OF GARDENING

YOU DON'T HAVE TO KNOW LATIN, BUT YOU DO HAVE TO SPEND MONEY

Have you ever suffered the embarrassment of asking the name of a pretty plant and then being told, *"Ajuga reptans?"* How much easier it would have been if your friend had simply answered, "carpet bugle." The plant looks like a carpet covering and, in the spring, it has blue spiked flowers that could conceivably remind one of bugles.

Unfortunately, what is known as carpet bugle in one area is called bugleweed in another, and who knows what else in a third. If you become serious about gardening, you will eventually find yourself—sometimes even against your will—having to learn the Latin or botanical names for plants. These names are accepted worldwide and precisely identify the plants. A botanical name in France is the same as that in Britain, the United States, Canada, Japan, or Australia. A common name in Britain, however, may not be the same as a common name in the United States. For example, the vegetables called zucchinis in the United States and Italy are called courgettes in Britain.

While there will come a day when you will find yourself using botanical names, this book will use the popular rather than the botanical names of plants wherever possible. You can find both names, however, in the index. For example, carpet bugle, bugleweed, and *Ajuga reptans* all appear in proper alphabetical order. Readers looking up the last two names, however, will be referred to the first, carpet bugle, which is used throughout the text.

There is one other very important aspect of gardening that should be discussed at this point: money. You will constantly be surprised at how much you are spending. Some expenses, such as buying tools and preparing the original flower bed, are one-time-only costs. Others are incurred infrequently, including the purchase of perennials that will bloom for many years. And still others occur every year, especially if you decide to buy annual flats.

In addition, you must be prepared for disaster. It happens to every gardener and the weekend practitioner should expect his or her fair share because he or she will not be there to water in a dry pinch or to nip a disease or an insect before it has a chance to spread. When calamity strikes, you have to spend money, either on new plants or on insecticides or fertilizers. This book does not give tips on how to save on garden expenses. The best advice may well be to keep the garden small if the budget is equally limited.

Above all, remember that gardening is fun. Don't take on more than you can enjoy. There is no such thing as a perfect garden—only perfect times for you as you work on your special weekend creation.

CHAPTER TWO

THE FOUR SEASONS OF THE GARDEN YEAR

The garden year is roughly equivalent to the four seasons of the temperate calendar year. During the winter months, you rest and store up energy in the form of plans for the warm months to come. It is the time of year for reading books such as this; browsing through catalogs with luscious, colored pictures of perfect flowers; sketching designs; and ordering plants for your garden.

In the spring, you are at your busiest—preparing the soil and, depending on the size of your garden, planting every weekend. Spring is an especially tricky time because it tends to rain a lot. Whole weekends can be washed away as far as the garden is concerned. For this reason, you might find yourself doing no garden chores one weekend and double time the next. The one compensating factor is that—if you were industrious the past fall—your garden is beckoning with bright yellow daffodils and other pretty bulbs, telling you that it's worth your effort to persevere.

If you follow the easy maintenance tips given in this book and pick up some of its simple design suggestions, you should find that the pace of work slackens considerably during the summer months. Your major chore will be watering during dry spells. This is the time of year to enjoy your garden, to pick its lovely flowers and to relish its fresh vegetables. As summer draws to a close, its heat may well lull you—turning your eye from any weeds or pests that have managed to invade your garden.

With the first blast of fall weather, however, all no-work excuses should be discarded immediately. This season is almost as busy as spring. It's a time for weeding vigorously and for cleaning thoroughly. These tasks deprive pests and insects of a refuge in which to winter over. This is also the

Flipping through catalogues is an enjoyable winter activity.

season for planting bulbs. Fall is, admittedly, a difficult time to be enthusiastic about gardening, but the hour or so you spend putting in bulbs like daffodils, tulips, or scilla will bring you more than triple the amount of enjoyment in flower viewing the next spring.

DREAMING AND CATALOGUE ORDERING

THE JOYS OF BEING AN ARMCHAIR GARDENER

Once the winter solstice and holiday season have ended, an enthusiastic sap seems to course through the veins of the gardener's imagination. It is the time of year when there are no nasty, crawling things to eat plants, no white or gray creatures to suck the life out of flowers, no fungi to blight the garden. All things seem possible in the grayness of winter, especially when one sits down to look at beautifully illustrated publications.

Somehow, at this time of year, you can believe that you too will have gardens and plants like those in the pictures. Reality never quite turns out that way, but you will find that your garden will be richer and more lively in the summer if you make an extra planning effort the previous winter. There are two, very simple design elements that you should remember in adding plants to your garden: 1) Try to have something blooming in your garden each season you are there; and, 2) have the taller plants in back and the shorter ones in front.

If the gardening sap level runs particularly high in your blood, you might want to go all out and do your planning right and proper. This means getting out chart and tissue or overlay paper and sketching in designs. First, draw an outline, to scale, of your garden. Then, again to scale, draw an approximate outline of where flowers are planted. Start with early spring and sketch in, for example, yellow where the daffodils are planted. The first tissue overlay could then contain red outlines for tulips, blue outlines for Jacob's ladder, and green outlines where the daffodils were once blooming. Continue adding overlays for the various bloom periods. This will give you an idea of the changing color scheme and the bare spots that may crop up in the garden.

Drawing colored circles and being meticulous may not be your cup of tea. If so, skip it. Just realize, however, that your garden will have some mismatches and empty spots during the summer. If at all possible, try to remember where these places are so that you can correct your mistakes the next year.

If you decide to buy your plants through a mail-order catalogue, you will find that each company supplies an order form that, at the very least, is less complicated than an income tax form. You will find the price of the plant next to its description. Be aware that prices differ dramatically from one nursery to the next. In the spring of 1985, for example, the mail-order price for three perennial bachelor's button plants at one nursery was over four times the price at another nursery.

There are many factors that go into the price differentials. Some have to do with quality of plants and some with quality of service and presentation. The more expensive nursery in the above example publishes a very complete catalogue that not only gives excellent descriptions of plants but also features essays on soil preparation, tools, fertilizers, and weed control. You pay for such extras and, in this case, you pay quite a bit.

While all nurseries ship plants at the appropriate planting time (so it doesn't matter how early you order), each has its own personality and philosophy. Your best bet at the beginning is to order from several different ones. The catalogues are very helpful in their own right, as many provide good pictures for plant identification and useful information about different plants. Once you've found the nursery that suits you best—in terms of plant quality, helpfulness of instructions, and price—stick with it.

PREPARING AND PLANTING
THE DIRTY ASPECT OF GARDENING

The well-known garden writer Amos Pettingill has a wonderful philosophy about garden soil: If it has green weeds, it also can have colorful flowers. Take a look at your potential garden spot. Is it nice and weedy? Then it should also be a good place for your garden. If you want to be absolutely on the safe side, however, contact your county agent or nearby agricultural college and ask them how you can go about testing your soil. Some may even test it for you, at a price, if you send samples. If you like, you can buy a fancy, expensive kit from your local nursery or via mail order and test for all sorts of soil ingredients yourself.

There's no question that if you start with good soil, your

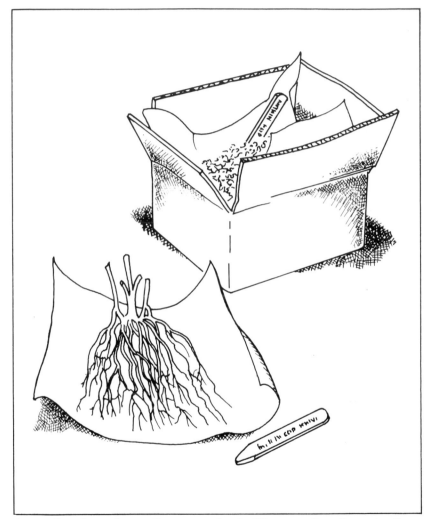

A mail-order plant does not look like much when it first arrives, but have faith! If you follow directions carefully and plant it as soon as you can, your reward will be lovely flowers later in the season.

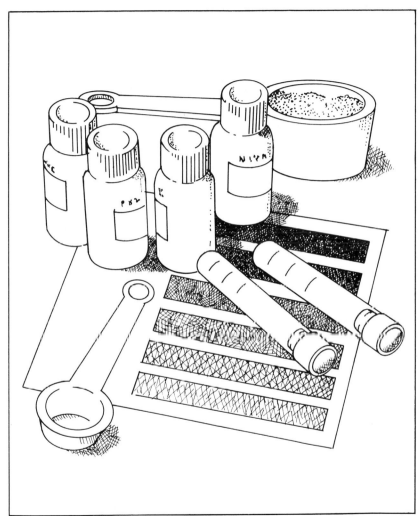

A soil-testing kit is a handy aid for the precise gardener who wants to increase his chance of success. They differ from pH kits, which only give readings on soil acidity, by testing for many soil nutrients.

chances of success are infinitely greater. It takes time and money, however, to turn a bed over with a pitchfork or spade, add sand, humus, or whatever else is needed to make it a rich soil that drains well and contains lots of organic matter. If you want to make such an effort, by all means do—the garden results will show it. This book, however, has attempted to make gardening life a little easier for you. While you will find that many flowers do need extra love and care in soil preparation, the plants listed in Appendix A should all do well in your garden with a minimum amount of soil preparation on your part.

One spring task that you really should undertake is determining your soil's acidity or, in scientific terms, pH. A pH reading of seven means your soil is neutral. Any number above seven indicates alkaline soil and a number lower than seven tells you that your soil is acidic. Most flowers grow best with a soil pH around six. There are all kinds of inexpensive testing kits at your local nursery. (These test pH only and are not as comprehensive as soil-testing kits.) The directions on the kit are quite easy to follow, and it takes no more than five minutes to get results. If your soil turns out to have a pH above seven, add peat moss or some other acid booster. If it has a pH well below six, add lime.

The only other major spring chore is planting seedlings. This is illustrated on page 36 and is as easy as it looks. Though you do have to get down on your hands and knees for this task, it can be one of the more pleasurable aspects of gardening. Working with warm soil, sensing a cool spring breeze ripple your hair, admiring the new seedlings—all can give a feeling of relaxation and of being attuned to the quiet, wonderous aspects of nature.

TRANSPLANTING

Though a simple task, transplanting must be done correctly.

(1) Be sure to dig a hole as deep as the seedling.

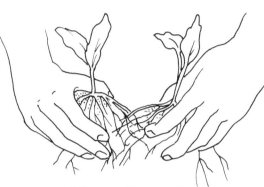

(2) If the seedlings all come in the same container, separate them very slowly at the roots.

(3) If the seedlings come in individual containers, peel the edge off and gently remove the seedling.

(4) Next, place the seedling in the hole.

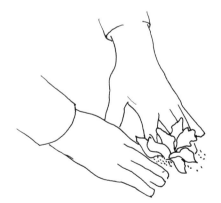

(5) Cover it with soil and firm it around.

(6) Water gently with a hose or a watering can.

Plant as early as possible during the weekend. If nights are not too cold, an early Friday evening would be perfect. Newly transplanted seedlings need lots of water to settle in, and you should give them a proper dousing Saturday morning, Sunday morning, and Sunday evening right before you leave. What to plant is, of course, up to you. The chart in this chapter should give you a rough idea of what you can expect to be in bloom during the various seasons. All the flowers are described in Appendix A.

While you're putting in new perennials and filling in bare spots with annuals, check on your daffodils. If they look a bit crowded, dig up about half the clump and transplant it to another part of the garden where you would like to have spring color. Make the bulbs happy in their new home by adding a dash of fertilizer. Or, dig up the bulbs once their green leaves have started turning brown and save them in a dry, dark spot until the fall planting.

Also, keep your eye out for any stray weeds that survived your fall cleaning. As Shakespeare wrote, "Now 'tis spring, and weeds are shallow-rooted; suffer them now and they'll o'ergrow the garden."

WATERING AND HARVESTING
THE PLEASURE OF YOUR OWN BOUNTY

There are three essentials for all plants: sun, soil, and water. You influence all three. You decided how much sun your plants would get when you picked your garden site; you

solved any soil problems during your spring chores; and you will find that during the dry summer months, watering will be your main and most crucial chore.

One way to minimize your work in this area is to mulch. Mulch, both a noun and a verb, refers to a covering—any kind—over the ground, and the act of putting the covering down. The mulch is spread over all parts of the garden where plants are not growing. (If you have a small garden, with plants close to one another, you will probably not need a mulch.) Once in place, the mulch keeps moisture from evaporating during dry spells.

The wonderful thing about mulch is that it smothers weeds as well. At the same time that it retains water in the ground, it also retains the tiny weed seedlings and never gives them the chance to reach the sun. As a weekend gardener, you must mulch because you will not be around your garden during the weekdays. And since you will also be knocking off weeds, you won't have to be concerned about weeding as a summer task.

There are all kinds of mulches—from your lawn's grass clippings to handsome, but expensive, items at your local nursery, such as wood chips, licorice root, and peat moss. Before you decide what to use, check to see what your local nursery has and how expensive it is. The nursery's experts also should tell you the advantages and disadvantages of the different mulches they offer.

If you opt for the inexpensive route and decide to use lawn clippings, you might be able to get extra ones from your neighbors. Be generous when you sprinkle the lawn clippings around your plants; up to two inches (five centimeters) thick is fine. In addition to being cheap, these also

Wood chips make a handsome and beneficial mulch.

Grass clippings are not as attractive, but they are a lot cheaper.

add good organic matter to your soil. Their main drawback is that as they dry, the clippings turn brown and are rather ugly. And, depending on the thickness, some will prevent water from reaching your plants' roots.

Even with a good mulch, however, it will be necessary to water during prolonged dry spells. Your plants will need a good watering at least once a week. Make sure the water goes down deep. A light sprinkle often does more harm than good because it will force roots upward in search of moisture, exposing them to harmful summer heat.

If your garden is small and you choose plants listed in Appendix A, insect pests should not be a major problem. Chapter Six reviews steps to take if pesky critters invade.

The only other major summer chore is snipping dead flower heads. Let them fall to the ground on Sunday afternoons. They add organic matter to the soil and will probably have shriveled up by the time you return the following weekend.

Once you've finished your watering and mulching (which shouldn't be that time-consuming), relax and enjoy your garden. Gardening is supposed to give you pleasure, and this time of year you should receive it in full measure.

CLEANING AND PLANTING
THE LAST GRUBBY, BUT ESSENTIAL, GARDEN BUSINESS OF THE YEAR

Cold autumn winds seem to tell you that it's time to go inside and curl up with a good book in front of a warm fire. Not so if you're a gardener! This is the time of year for a last bout of activity. After the annuals and many of the perennials have been laid low by an early frost, check to see what hardy weeds remain and get to work in pulling them out immediately. Weeds are loaded with seeds at this time of year and ache to produce hundreds of descendants to vex you next summer. Fall is the time to keep them from nature's appointed task. Extend yourself and spend a good weekend or two getting rid of any weeds and cleaning your garden thoroughly.

This is also the time of year to review quite clinically all the plants in your garden. Have they performed up to expectation? Have they been strong and hardy? If not, get rid of them. It's a cruel, Darwinian world, and if you want any sort of decent weekend garden with a minimum amount of work, get rid of weak and diseased plants. You do not have the time to give them the nurture they need.

Throw away all debris from plants that have been knocked down by frost. If you give your garden a good fall cleaning, pests do not have a chance to winter over.

Once your garden is neat and tidy, think about planting some bulbs. This is the time of year to do it and, next spring, you will be so glad that you did. Before you drop the bulb in the hole, be sure to mix in at the bottom a teaspoon or so of bone meal (the name sounds like a ghoulish mixture, but actually it's a fertilizer that you can buy at your local nursery).

By now, cold weather has probably arrived and it's time for you to take your winter rest, to congratulate yourself on the garden year's successes, and to slowly germinate plans for next year's triumphs.

Toward the end of the garden year, review each plant's performance critically. Without mercy, throw away the weak and the sick.

A REFERENCE GUIDE FOR FLOWERS, BY SEASON AND HEIGHT

This chart should help you plan your garden according to the bloom period of the flowers and the height of the plant. All bloom periods are approximate and are based on a climate where the temperature varies from five below zero (minus twenty degrees Celsius) to ninety-five degrees (thirty-five degrees Celsius). Some plants have extended flowering periods and are listed under several seasons; others, like marigolds, come in different heights and are listed under different height categories. An indication is given of the range of colors for each flower, so you can be sure the plants you choose complement and contrast with each other in the way you want them to. All of the plants below are described in greater detail in Appendix A.

BLOOM PERIOD	HEIGHT			BLOOM PERIOD	HEIGHT		
	SHORT less than one foot (30 cms.)	MEDIUM one to two feet (30 to 60 cms.)	TALL two to three feet (60 to 90 cms.)		SHORT less than one foot (30 cms.)	MEDIUM one to two feet (30 to 60 cms.)	TALL two to three feet (60 to 90 cms.)
LATE WINTER	SNOWDROP white CROCUS white, blue, purple, yellow SIBERIAN SQUILL [SCILLA] blue			MID- TO LATE SPRING	AGERATUM blue BEGONIA white through red BROWALLIA blue CANDYTUFT white CARPET BUGLE blue CHIVES lavender LILY OF THE VALLEY white MARIGOLD white, red, yellow PANSY white, purple, yellow	DAFFODIL white, yellow BLEEDING HEART pink BUGLOSS blue COLUMBINE white through dark purple IMPATIENS white through red JACOB'S LADDER blue MARIGOLD white, red, yellow PETUNIA almost all colors SPANISH SCILLA blue SUNDROP yellow	SIBERIAN IRIS blue, pink PEONY white, pink
EARLY- TO MID-SPRING	BISHOP'S HAT pink PANSY white, purple, yellow	DAFFODIL white, yellow VIRGINIA BLUEBELLS blue BLEEDING HEART pink JACOB'S LADDER blue					

BLOOM PERIOD	HEIGHT			BLOOM PERIOD	HEIGHT		
	SHORT less than one foot (30 cms.)	**MEDIUM** one to two feet (30 to 60 cms.)	**TALL** two to three feet (60 to 90 cms.)		**SHORT** less than one foot (30 cms.)	**MEDIUM** one to two feet (30 to 60 cms.)	**TALL** two to three feet (60 to 90 cms.)
EARLY TO MID-SUMMER	**AGERATUM** blue **BEGONIA** white through red **BROWALLIA** blue **MARIGOLD** white, red, yellow **PANSY** white, purple, yellow **SWEET ALYSSUM** white	**ASTILBE** white through red **BACHELOR'S BUTTON** blue **CELOSIA** red, gold, purple **CORAL BELL** white through red **COREOPSIS** yellow **DAY LILY** yellow, red **FEVERFEW** white **GERANIUM** white through red **IMPATIENS** white through red **MARIGOLD** white, red, yellow **PAINTED DAISY** white through red **PETUNIA** almost all colors **POT MARIGOLD** yellow **SALVIA** red **SUNDROP** yellow **YARROW** red	**BALLOON FLOWER** blue, pink, white **BEE BALM** purple, pink, red **BLACK-EYED SUSAN** yellow **DAY LILY** yellow, red **MARIGOLD** white, red, yellow **SPIDERWORT** white, blue, pink	**MID- TO LATE SUMMER**	**AGERATUM** blue **BEGONIA** white through red **BROWALLIA** blue **MARIGOLD** white, red, yellow **SWEET ALYSSUM** white	**BACHELOR'S BUTTON** blue **CELOSIA** red, purple, gold **CHRYSANTHEMUM** almost all colors **CORAL BELL** white through red **COREOPSIS** yellow **DAY LILY** yellow, red **FEVERFEW** white **GERANIUM** white through red **IMPATIENS** white through red **MARIGOLD** white, red, yellow **PETUNIA** almost all colors **POT MARIGOLD** yellow **SALVIA** red **SEDUM** pink	**BALLOON FLOWER** blue, pink, white **BEE BALM** purple, red, pink **BLACK-EYED SUSAN** yellow **CHRYSANTHEMUM** almost all colors **DAY LILY** yellow, red **MARIGOLD** white, red, yellow **PERENNIAL AGERATUM** blue **SPIDERWORT** white, blue, pink
				FALL	**CANDYTUFT** white **SWEET ALYSSUM** white	**CHRYSANTHEMUM** almost all colors **FEVERFEW** white **POT MARIGOLD** yellow	**BLACK-EYED SUSAN** yellow **CHRYSANTHEMUM** almost all colors

CHAPTER THREE

THREE
SHADE GARDENS

One of the earliest botany lessons children learn is that chlorophyll is the pigment that makes plants green. Its function is to absorb light for photosynthesis, the process through which plants manufacture food and oxygen from water and carbon dioxide. If there were no light, there would be no green plants.

And yet, there are shade gardens. It almost seems a contradiction in terms for, by definition, shade means sheltered from sunlight. These types of gardens are possible because of the wonderful adaptability of plants. Built-in genetic characteristics allow some green plants to exist with only one-tenth the light needed by sun-loving flowers.

There are, of course, varying degrees of shade. In this book, partial shade is used to describe places that receive some sun during the day (no more than four or five hours) and are in shade the rest of the day. Dappled shade, on the other hand, refers to a spot that only gets sun as it is filtered through trees. And full shade refers to areas—such as those under a maple tree or on the north side of a house—that do not get any sunlight during the day.

The amount of shade any one spot gets varies by season. For example, an area that is in full shade during the summer can be in full sun before tree leaves come out in the spring. That's one reason why crocuses and early daffodils are so popular; they add spring color to a spot that is in full shade by the middle of the summer. Garden areas that are shady in the spring because the sun is low receive quite a bit of light when the sun is at its summer height. Make your gardening life easier by checking when you want your plants to bloom and then seeing what kind of shade the garden area has at that time of year.

For some reason, shade seems to stump many gardeners, putting them at a loss as to what to grow. As shown in the table, there are many plants that can grow in shade; some, in fact, prefer it. Careful readers will note, however, that there is a striking difference between the plants listed under full shade and those under partial shade: in general, the more shade, the less likelihood the plant will bear a colorful flower (fortunately, impatiens and begonias are exceptions). Most plants have to put so much energy into just surviving without sunlight that there is little left over for producing colorful blossoms.

Some plants seem to compensate for lack of bloom, however, by producing variegated foliage. The green-and-white leaves of some hostas serve as a good example. Two of the more popular varieties are: *Hosta undulata,* which tends to have white in the center and green on the outside of the leaves, and *Hosta albo marginata*—known as white edge hosta—which has a reverse color scheme. As the degree of shade lessens, the setting seems more hospitable for plants to take on more color. Usually, these are quiet, cool colors like white, pink, light blue, and pale yellow.

It is this quality—lack of a range of colors—that makes a shade garden so challenging. Gardeners seek a variety of leaf shapes instead, and the result can be as pleasing and refreshing as the most splendid of sun gardens.

If you have a shady location for your weekend garden, here are some tips on what plants to include. The first two examples show what can be done with full or dappled shade, and the second illustrates how you can have a changing color pattern with partial shade. All the plants in the gardens are described in greater detail in Appendix A.

Here is a lazy gardener's ideal garden. The plants survive on their own, needing only an occasional check to ensure they are not spreading too much.

You do not need many plants to make an attractive arrangement in a small, shady spot. The compact garden in the example contains just four plants—carpet bugle, hosta, fern, and iris. Best of all, these plants will grow without any help from you.

TWO GREEN GARDENS
COOLING OFF IN SHADE

In the high heat of summer, a dark, green oasis of plants seems, at least psychologically, refreshing and restful. This section describes two such gardens.

The first represents the kind you can tuck in a small area, say between two bushes. It is six feet (two meters) long and three feet (90 centimeters) deep. It has only four kinds of plants: carpet bugle, ferns, hosta, and iris. The carpet bugle will send forth blue spikes in mid-spring and the hosta blue flowers on long stems in mid-summer. Aside from these two blue splashes, the garden will be without flowers for the rest of the growing season.

Yet, what a nice little spot it is. The green-and-white hosta occupies the center of attention. The carpet bugle covers the ground in front of it with dark green leaves. To the side, delicate and airy ferns gently waft the hosta, and, in back, the long slender iris foliage guards the hosta from the rear. The iris, in fact, is included in this scheme solely for its long, elegant leaves. There is not enough sun for it to produce flowers. If your garden is in exceptionally deep shade, the iris might not even produce enough foliage to be effective; eliminate it and put more ferns in its place.

This is the kind of garden that has to sink or swim on its own. There is, literally, no weekly maintenance. That means no mulching, weeding, or watering. The leaves of the carpet bugle and hosta not only act as mulch in their own right but also smother any weeds that try to become established in their territory. The plants are all tough, and at least some should survive if your garden suffers a prolonged drought. If you wanted, you could leave this garden for a year and come back and still find it there.

You don't get away scot-free, however: at least once a year, you should check to make sure that the carpet bugle, ferns, and hosta are not spreading too much. If they are, just yank up the unwanted intruders. Carpet bugle, in particular, can be pesty, having a decided tendency to march forward into your lawn.

When using carpet bugle or any other invasive plant as a border, it is best to put in a metal or plastic lawn edging. This is a strip of material about four inches (nine centimeters) high that serves as a barrier between your lawn and your garden when it is pushed into the earth along the garden's edge. You can buy it at your local nursery or through some of the mail-order catalogs. Complete installation instructions come on its package.

The second garden is much larger and more suited for partial shade, although you can try it in full shade. Triangular in shape, it measures six feet (180 centimeters) along the short sides and about nine feet (240 centimeters) along the diagonal. It contains the following plants: bishop's hat, bleeding heart, hosta, iris, lily of the valley, and yellow archangel. It is built around a large bush or shrub, such as a rhododendron, that anchors the spot.

Once again, color is second to leaf shape in the visual appreciation of the garden. This design aspect of gardening was stressed by Beatrix Farrand, the first of America's eminent female landscape gardeners and a contemporary of Britain's Gertrude Jekyll. In her gardens for such clients as the Rockefellers at Seal Harbor, Maine, and the Blisses at Dunbarton Oaks at Washington, D.C., Farrand would work out the texture scheme of the leaves before even considering the colors and kinds of flowers.

While weekend gardeners do not have the time to review the shape of each leaf in their gardens, at least a passing thought should be given to this aspect of gardening, particularly if the garden is shaded. As shown on page 48, the leaves in this garden arrangement offer quite a contrast, an effect attained by using very common garden plants. You should be able to get a similar effect in your garden.

Color is not totally neglected in this garden, and you will find quite a bit of it in spring—pink flowers from the bishop's hat and bleeding heart, white from the lily of the valley, and yellow from the appropriately named yellow archangel. In mid-summer, the two green hosta clumps at the corners will put forth blue flowers. For the rest of the season, however, the varying foliages—highlighted by the

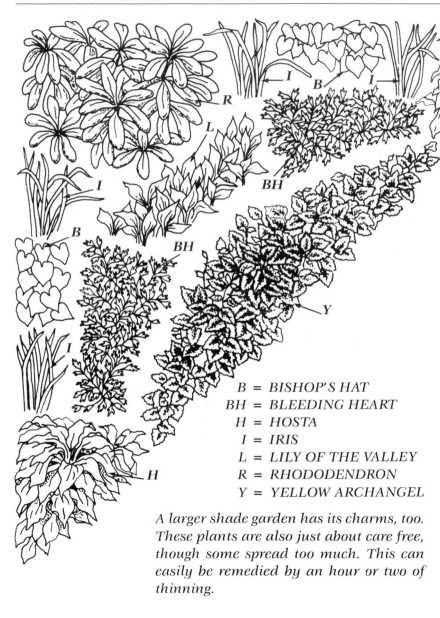

B = BISHOP'S HAT
BH = BLEEDING HEART
H = HOSTA
I = IRIS
L = LILY OF THE VALLEY
R = RHODODENDRON
Y = YELLOW ARCHANGEL

A larger shade garden has its charms, too. These plants are also just about care free, though some spread too much. This can easily be remedied by an hour or two of thinning.

The texture scheme of leaves is an important design consideration, particularly for shade gardens. The leaves shown here, taken from the plants illustrated in the garden on the left, present some of the variety available.

silver and green of the yellow archangel—are the chief attraction of this garden.

As with the smaller shade garden, the only maintenance requirement here is keeping the plants in their assigned area. If you find them straying, just pull them up and either throw them away or give them a new home elsewhere in your garden. If you feel terribly energetic, a good weekly watering of the bleeding heart will give you a summer of bloom. If that seems like too much work, however, skip this chore and just enjoy the plant for its lovely, feathery foliage.

This drawing with the next two shows how you can have changing color schemes in a garden. In the spring, this garden consists of blues and yellows.

A FLOWER GARDEN

COLORING PARTIAL SHADE

This relatively simple garden—there are only ten different kinds of plants—illustrates the fun you can have with color schemes. While the green gardens just discussed empha-sized the importance of leaf texture, there are those who feel color takes precedence over all clsc in thc garden.

Color, to these enthusiasts, has all sorts of beneficial effects. At the turn of the century, for example, F. W. Miles, the Head Gardener at Britain's Ware Park, wrote: "The importance of proper colour-blending in the garden...is

By mid-summer, the color scheme has changed to pink and white with attractive clumps of green foliage scattered throughout.

health giving, for it has been well and fully stated that few people realize the effect colour has on the course of one's life and character."

Miles also felt that in a small garden there should be no attempt to display a range of colors (bad for the health, one supposes). He argued instead that only two or three colors should be used. Gertrude Jekyll agreed with this approach and took it one step further, saying that separate gardens should be set aside, each for its own time of year, and each properly coordinated with regard to color.

The gardens illustrated in Chapter Four totally disregard the separation of color principle espoused by Miles and

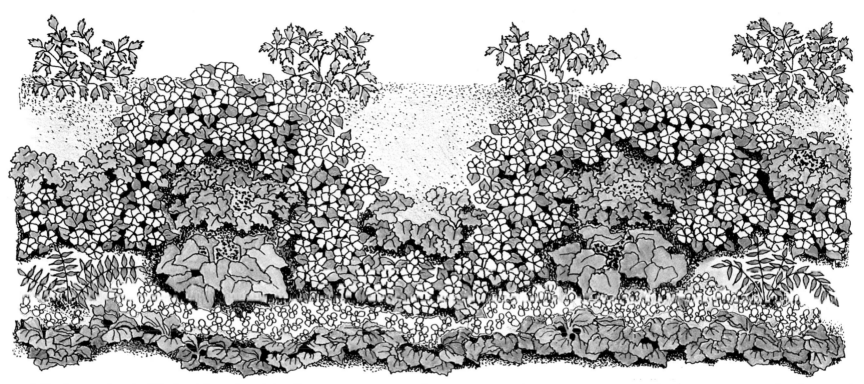

By fall, the garden is filled with only white flowers. Impatiens plants are quite large at this time and form a dramatic background.

Miss Jekyll. For those who would like to get some idea of how this theory works, however, the following partial shade garden is offered. Since this book assumes the reader does not have the space or time that Miss Jekyll did, the garden is a three-season one, with each season having its own color scheme. This is not a large garden, measuring only six feet (two meters) by ten feet (three meters), but it is a carefully coordinated one.

In the spring, the garden consists of cheery yellows and blues—a treat after the white and grayness of winter. The border of yellow and blue crocuses blooms first, followed shortly afterward by the early yellow daffodils. The foliage

SOME PLANTS FOR YOUR SHADE GARDEN

The plants in this list should give you some idea of the range of possibilities you have in planning a shade garden. All are described in greater detail in Appendix A.

PARTIAL SHADE	DAPPLED SHADE	FULL SHADE
AGERATUM	AGERATUM	—
ASTILBE	ASTILBE	—
BEE BALM	BEE BALM	—
BEGONIA	BEGONIA	BEGONIA
BISHOP'S HAT	BISHOP'S HAT	BISHOP'S HAT
BLEEDING HEART	BLEEDING HEART	BLEEDING HEART
BROWALLIA	BROWALLIA	—
BUGLOSS	BUGLOSS	—
CARPET BUGLE	CARPET BUGLE	CARPET BUGLE
COLEUS	COLEUS	COLEUS
COLUMBINE	COLUMBINE	—
CORAL BELL	CORAL BELL	—
DAY LILY	DAY LILY	—
FERN	FERN	FERN
HOSTA	HOSTA	HOSTA
IMPATIENS	IMPATIENS	IMPATIENS
JACOB'S LADDER	JACOB'S LADDER	—
LILY OF THE VALLEY	LILY OF THE VALLEY	LILY OF THE VALLEY
PACHYSANDRA	PACHYSANDRA	PACHYSANDRA
PERIWINKLE	PERIWINKLE	PERIWINKLE
SIBERIAN IRIS	SIBERIAN IRIS	—
SPIDERWORT	SPIDERWORT	—
YELLOW ARCHANGEL	YELLOW ARCHANGEL	YELLOW ARCHANGEL

of the latter should be tied after the bloom period, so that the blue scilla behind can be seen easily. Late yellow daffodils should constitute a bright barrier between the blue scilla plants. These will be followed by the blue flowers on the Jacob's ladder and the bugloss.

By early summer, the color scheme has totally changed and is now pink and white, with some nice green foliage clumps provided by the Jacob's ladder and bugloss. The pink coral bells will bloom first and will last almost two months. They will be joined by the exotic pink blossoms of the bee balm and the elegant spires of white astilbe. This is the only time you will have to work hard in this garden because the design now calls for the planting of white impatiens and begonia seedlings.

By the fall, the garden is all white. The impatiens plants grow quite large and should make a dramatic backdrop to the lower-growing white begonias.

This garden requires a bit more work than the first two discussed. Since the plants do not spread as much, it will be necessary to mulch in order to cut down on your watering chores and eliminate weeds. You might also find, if your summers are hot and humid, that the bee balm will be covered with mildew after its bloom period. If this is the case, simply cut the stems to the ground and throw them away. The plants should recover and bloom as beautifully for the next year.

"Hide me from the day's garish eye," the poet John Milton wrote, and this is what your shade garden offers you: a quiet, cool retreat. This kind of garden is heavily oriented toward perennials and, once established, requires little work on your part. Enjoy its peace and calm.

CHAPTER FOUR

THREE FLOWER GARDENS

In the first chapter of this book, you were asked to decide which flowers you wanted in your garden, during what seasons you wanted them in bloom, and how large you wanted your garden. This chapter will give you some suggestions on how to implement your decisions if you have a spot that gets at least six hours of sun each day. As mentioned before, all plants in these garden schemes are covered in greater detail in the appendixes. For every plant that you may consider, you will find a description of its height, bloom period, and color—as well as any drawbacks or positive features—in the back of the book.

Three gardens are presented. In each case, one garden bed serves as the setting for spring, summer, and fall flowers. This kind of plan, as the famous English gardener Gertrude Jekyll wrote over half a century ago, greatly restricts the choice of plants, as well as their designs. Often, you will see pictures of beautiful spring gardens loaded with daffodils, tulips, azalea, and scilla. Have you ever thought of what those gardens look like in summer or fall? An oasis of cool green, perhaps, but certainly not of color.

The schemes given in this chapter presume that the weekend gardener has neither the time nor the space to set up separate gardens for the different seasons of the year. Seasonal growing schemes are all combined under one garden roof, so to speak. While this does have its restrictions, it also provides ease of maintenance and lots of creative challenge.

There is only one farily consistent design element in all three gardens: Tall plants go to the back and short ones to the front. This seems so obvious that one could legitimately ask why the point was raised. Here's the answer: Many

people neglect to consider height when putting in flowers. Whenever you buy a plant, make sure you know how tall it will be when it reaches full height, and try to remember how tall the other plants are that will be growing around it.

The first garden is an informal one and shows how you can pack a lot of plants into a relatively small space. Because the garden is heavily weighted with perennials, you will find yourself welcomed with a new configuration of color and shape each weekend. You will also have the opportunity to be creative in your cut-flower arrangements because you will have different flowers to work with just about every weekend. A few annuals give this garden a touch of continuity throughout the summer and fall.

The second garden is the easiest, quickest, and initially the most expensive of the three. It contains a few bulbs for spring color and a lovely formal arrangement of just four different flowers that last all summer and into the early fall. This garden consists primarily of annuals, and about the only maintenance that is required is weekly watering.

The last garden is a large informal grouping of a relatively limited number of plants—less, in fact, than the number contained in the first garden. This is designed to show you that it is possible to have a big garden without having to learn about a lot of different plants and without having to do a lot of weekend chores. With the exception of the marigolds, this garden consists entirely of tough perennials that are meant to thrive on their own.

An easy weekend garden would be one consisting of day lilies; there are enough different varieties to provide blooms all summer.

A SMALL INFORMAL GARDEN

PACKING IT ALL IN

This is a truly informal garden. Its design scheme is similar to taking several cans of different-colored paints and throwing them at a canvas: lots of colors, but no particular order. The colors—red, purple, yellow, orange, pink, blue, and white—come from thirty different kinds of plants. Because many of these are perennials that do not bloom all year long, some of the space will be in bloom some of the time, but not all of the garden all of the time. There will, however, always be a spot of color to welcome you to your weekend retreat during the warmer months of the year.

A small group of purple crocuses starts off the garden year in this scheme. Throughout the bed, you'll find daffodil shoots with their promise of spring color to come. The daffodils are different varieties, some blooming early and some late. This means you can have fresh-cut daffodils for the weekend for at least six weeks.

Just to get you and the garden in the proper mood, a border row of pansies is included in the design. Pansies can be bought in flats from your local nursery in late winter or early spring. They do best in cool weather and will even survive light frosts. Plant them as early as they are available; if they don't survive, you can always get another flat.

Spring is a good time to check the garden to see if any stray weeds are left over from last year. You can probably spot these when you're planting your pansies and easily dig them up.

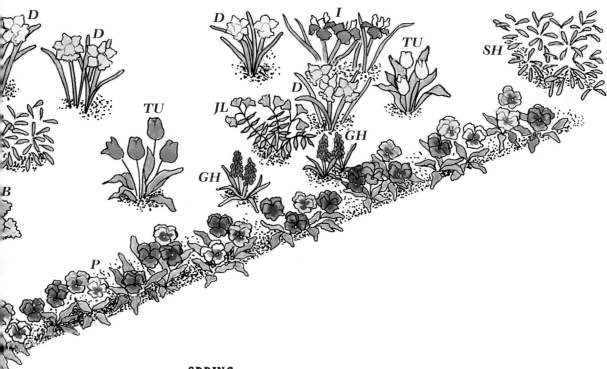

This drawing and the next two illustrate how you can cram a lot of different flowers into a relatively small space. Pictured here is the garden in spring. It is filled with sturdy, colorful perennials, which means little work for you. Indeed, your only chore is to plant a row of bright, cheery pansies.

SPRING

CB = *CORAL BELLS*
CR = *CROCUS*
CT = *CANDYTUFT*
 D = *DAFFODIL*
GH = *GRAPE HYACINTH*
 I = *IRIS*
JL = *JACOB'S LADDER*
 P = *PANSEY*
RB = *ROSE BUSH*
SH = *SHASTA DAISY*
TU = *TULIPS*

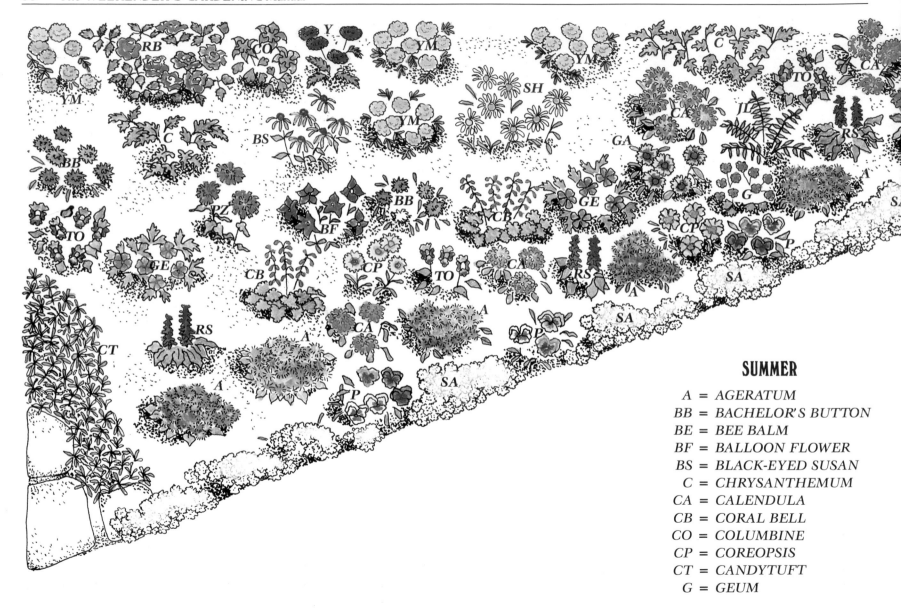

SUMMER

A = AGERATUM
BB = BACHELOR'S BUTTON
BE = BEE BALM
BF = BALLOON FLOWER
BS = BLACK-EYED SUSAN
C = CHRYSANTHEMUM
CA = CALENDULA
CB = CORAL BELL
CO = COLUMBINE
CP = COREOPSIS
CT = CANDYTUFT
G = GEUM

Most annual flowers will bloom for a long period of time. In the summer garden pictured here, blue ageratum, white alyssum, red salvia, pink zinnias, and yellow marigolds add colorful splashes all through the growing season while various perennial blossoms burst forth, then fade away. Your biggest job during this usually dry time of year is to make sure your plants have enough water.

GA = GAILLARDA
GE = GERANIUM
JL = JACOB'S LADDER
 P = PANSEY
PZ = PINK ZINNIA
RB = ROSE BUSH
RS = RED SALVIA
SA = SWEET ALYSSUM
SH = SHASTA DAISY
TO = TORENIA
 Y = YARROW
YM = YELLOW MARIGOLD

Believe it or not, that is the end of the spring garden chores for this garden. The remaining plants are perennials and are accustomed to surviving with only the care that nature provides at this time of year.

Once the spring rains are over and the last frost date is behind you, it is time to get busy again and fill in spots of the garden with annuals. In all probability, at least some of the pansies will have started to fade in the summer heat. At the same time, the sweet alyssum from last year has left hundreds of tiny seeds in the garden; these respond to the rains and the warmth and are now forming a border of tiny plants—without the gardener having to do any work at all. (If you didn't plant sweet alyssum last year, make sure you do this year.)

In this garden scheme, blue ageratum plants are put behind the white alyssum; red salvia and pink zinnia are planted behind the ageratum. Wishbone flowers and tall yellow marigolds are scattered throughout the garden wherever there is a bare spot.

It is best not to plant all the annuals at once, but rather one or two flats a weekend. The problem is water. Seedlings need lots of it, and you want to make sure the first batch have survived before you go to the nursery to get the second batch the following weekend. If at all possible, do your planting on Friday evening or early Saturday morning. This gives seedlings a day or two to settle in before you have to leave them.

All that is left of your daffodils and tulips are the green leaves, which add nothing to the flower garden, so you might be tempted to cut them now. Don't! They do add nourishment for next year's flowers, and for this reason

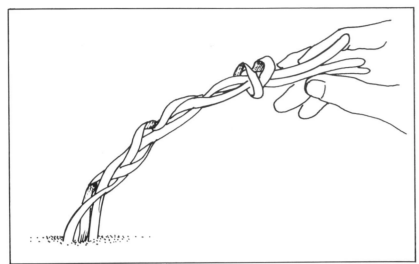

Unattractive daffodil foliage can be partially concealed by braiding.

must be allowed to follow through on their natural course. The daffodil leaves can be put down a peg or two by being tied; just braid them as you would a pigtail and fold them over, or tie them in a knot. Either way, the height of the leaves is cut by about half. There's not much you can do about the tulip foliage, which is why only three clumps are included in the design scheme. By mid-summer, however, the foliage of both the tulip and the daffodil will have disappeared.

Once you have finished planting the annuals, your weekly tasks for this garden consist simply of watering liberally and keeping an eye out for weeds, diseases, and insect pests. There should be few weeds because the garden is so small and covered with other plants. Again, because of

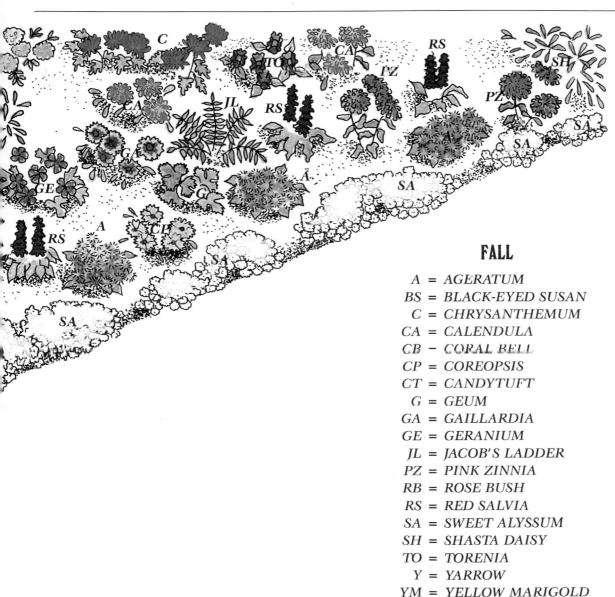

In the fall garden pictured here, the color scheme becomes more subdued as many of the brighter annuals finally peter out. This is a time for warm colors—reds, yellows, and bronzes—harbingers of cozy times in front of a fireplace in the months to come. Yet, while the colors lure you to the fire, the garden does not! This is a busy time of year for weeding and cleaning up the garden.

FALL

A = AGERATUM
BS = BLACK-EYED SUSAN
C = CHRYSANTHEMUM
CA = CALENDULA
CB = CORAL BELL
CP = COREOPSIS
CT = CANDYTUFT
G = GEUM
GA = GAILLARDIA
GE = GERANIUM
JL = JACOB'S LADDER
PZ = PINK ZINNIA
RB = ROSE BUSH
RS = RED SALVIA
SA = SWEET ALYSSUM
SH = SHASTA DAISY
TO = TORENIA
Y = YARROW
YM = YELLOW MARIGOLD

its size, insect and disease infestation should also be relatively slight and easy to handle.

This garden is so small and the plants so packed together that you will probably find it unnecessary to mulch. Mulch, as described in Chapter Two, is a covering put on the ground that conserves moisture and smothers weeds. If you want to mulch here, by all means do so. On the other hand, if you don't want to invest the time and effort, don't feel guilty about your laziness.

You should find this garden quite lovely in the summer; a burst of brilliant color will greet you every weekend. There will be yellow-and-black black-eyed Susans, bright orange geum, purple bee balm, yellow marigolds, and much more. Every weekend will be different because as one perennial ceases to bloom another will start.

When cooler days and shorter nights announce the imminent arrival of fall, it is time to get busy again. Cut down the foliage of perennials that have finished blooming, check to see if there are any weeds lurking about and promptly remove them. Trim those plants—such as gaillardia—that are still blooming but look leggy and ungainly. Keep an eye out for perennials that are spreading beyond their allotted boundaries in this small garden. Yank back those that wander. This may sound like a lot of work, but it should all be accomplished within two hours on a weekend.

The garden now will be a bit subdued, but there should still be color—mostly red, yellow, and bronze—that will last through a light frost or two. One good way of covering up some of the bare spots resulting from your cleanup is to plunk down pots of chrysanthemums wherever the garden is particularly drab. These pots will have to be thrown away eventually because in all probability there are perennials below the surface; nevertheless, it is worth the expense to have the extra color and life at this time of year.

A SMALL FORMAL GARDEN
KEEPING IT BRIGHT AND SIMPLE

The garden described here is based on one designed by Alan Goodheart, a member of the American Society of Landscape Architects. Mr. Goodheart likes to design gardens, and he likes to admire gardens; he does not, however, like to work in gardens, especially during his free time. He came up with a perfect solution for a weekend gardener who wants color, simple design, and no work except an occasional watering.

As discussed in Chapter Two, good soil can make life a lot easier for the flower gardener. Mr. Goodheart, favoring the easy life, bought the soil for his garden. First, however, he drew a circle twelve feet (four meters) in diameter and thirty-eight feet (eleven and a half meters) in circumference, and removed a layer of soil about six inches (fifteen centimeters) deep from within the circle. In its place, he dumped a load of topsoil. He had requested the smallest amount possible from a local nursery; the little that was left over was added to his vegetable garden. Mr. Goodheart smoothed the soil out so that it formed a half-oval mound, with the highest point about eight inches above ground level in the center. (If you have a particularly clayey soil

This formal garden is elegant and simple. In the spring, easy-to-grow bulb plants ensure that there is little or no work to be done.

that does not drain well, Mr. Goodheart recommends that you dig your initial hole about one and a half feet [forty-five centimeters] deep. In the lower part, mix soil and gravel—also bought from the nursery—about one foot [thirty centimeters] deep, then put the topsoil above this layer.)

For spring color, he planted a row of crocuses around the circumference, a circle of snowdrops about halfway up the mound, and daffodils at the top and at each quarter point of the circumference. When the last possible frost date had

passed, he went back to the nursery and bought flats of four different annuals: sweet alyssum, ageratum, marigolds, and salvia. That was expensive, but Mr. Goodheart felt it was worth it. He and his wife, Carol (at times like this, it's nice to have someone to share chores with), planted the seedlings and mulched with licorice root, an attractive, organic covering that also was bought at the nursery. At the end of the afternoon, the Goodhearts had an instant garden and instant color. Their only garden chores for the remainder of

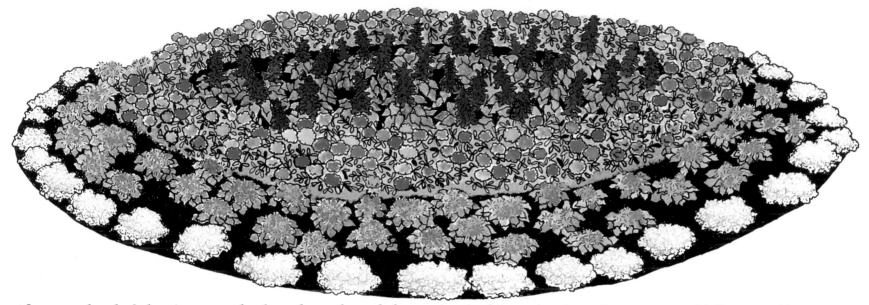

After a weekend of planting annuals, the only work needed to maintain this garden through summer and fall is a weekly watering.

the summer were watering during prolonged dry spells and snipping off the seed heads of the ageratum and marigolds to encourage further bloom.

A LARGE INFORMAL GARDEN

SPREADING IT ALL OUT

While there is something charming about a small, colorful garden, there is something grand about a sweep of plants that borders a large area. This garden illustrates one way you can obtain such grandeur with a minimum amount of work. There are only twenty plants in this garden, but there are large clumps of each, and they pick up and complement each other throughout the cycle of flowering.

As mentioned earlier in this book, buying plants can be expensive. If you would like a garden of this size, it might be best to start out small and then, as the perennial plants spread each year, gradually transplant them to the expanded garden space.

Plants in this garden are allowed to roam at will. If you don't like what you see, just pull them up and either discard or put them in a place where you would prefer them to be. This kind of a garden is a continual surprise, not only throughout the growing season as different plants bloom but also from year to year as the plants spread and reseed themselves throughout the growing area.

But even with all the freedom given the plants, some restrictions are imposed. Daffodils, for example, are planted in a long curving line to tie in the various sections of the garden. As with the small, informal garden, different varieties are planted so that there is a long bloom period. Once the daffodils have ceased to bloom, a wide swath of marigolds are planted. These also add a curving line to tie various parts of the garden together.

In the front of the garden, clumps of candytuft and hosta are planted. These act as garden guards, letting the onlooker know exactly where the garden begins and where the lawn may not intrude. One corner of the garden is anchored with peonies. (The peonies look particularly dramatic when planted on a mound of dirt six inches [fifteen centimeters] high; this touch is not a must, however.) The green foliage of the peonies adds a nice backdrop to the color of the remaining plants during the summer months.

About one quarter of the garden is given over to a day lily bed. These bloom at different times throughout the summer. In fact, the ultimate in a low-maintenance garden would be a continuous border of day lilies. Since these come in just about all colors and heights, one could have flowers in bloom from late spring through the end of summer and literally do no work at all after the initial planting.

The major chores that you really should undertake with a garden of this size are mulching (described in Chapter Two), watering, controlling diseases and pests, trimming seed heads, and thinning overgrown clumps. If you like, you can spend additional time transplanting, weeding, and cleaning up. The garden can be as informal (in this case, that means messy) or as neat as you like.

Watering such a large garden is a big job. The garden, however, incorporates many plants that can at least survive, if not do well, in drought. These are black-eyed Susan, bleeding heart, chrysanthemum, chive, candytuft, day lily, feverfew, hosta, bee balm, sedum, and (when not in bloom) sundrop. Rather than try to water the whole area every weekend, apply the hose or watering can selectively to the marigolds and those plants that look like they need it the most (and then pray mightily for rain during the next week).

As described in Chapter Six, it is essential to tend to a sick plant at once and to clean the garden in the fall. This garden is so large that it is bound to feel ill in some places at some times. You should check it carefully every weekend to make sure the plants are healthy and, when they aren't, take corrective action immediately.

Trimming seed heads should take no more than an hour each month; it is wise not to skip this task. All you need is a pair of scissors. Just snip off the flower head and leave it on the ground if you are not scrupulously neat and tidy. The old flower will decay and add organic matter to your soil. Trim the faded flowers of daffodils so that they will not go to seed and deter flower growth the next year. Cut the faded heads of bachelor's buttons, balloon flowers, black-eyed

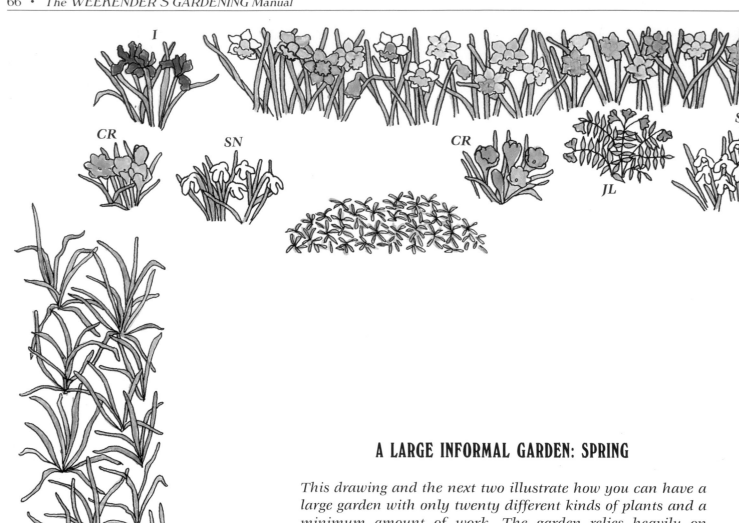

A LARGE INFORMAL GARDEN: SPRING

This drawing and the next two illustrate how you can have a large garden with only twenty different kinds of plants and a minimum amount of work. The garden relies heavily on sturdy perennials. These are planted in large clumps or long sweeps throughout. Most of these perennials spread, giving you extra plants each year to move and change the design scheme to suit your fancy.

FLOWERS IN BLOOM

BH = BLEEDING HEART
CH = CHIVES
CR = CROCUS
 D = DAFFODIL
 I = IRIS
JL = JACOB'S LADDER
 P = PEONY
SN = SNOWDROP

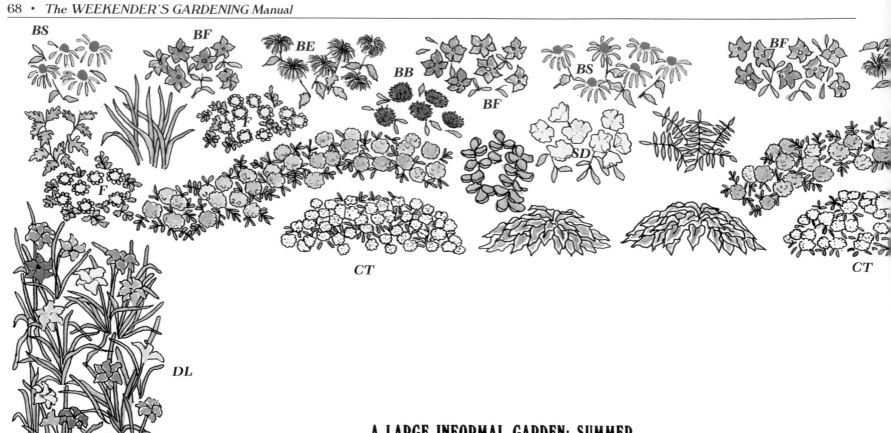

A LARGE INFORMAL GARDEN: SUMMER

In order to ensure some continuous color in this design, marigolds are planted in a long row in early summer. These are the only annuals in this garden.

Mulching is an absolute necessity. If you neglect this task, you might find sweeps of weeds rather than flowers. Pests and disease also have room to lurk here, so you will need to check your plants carefully every week to catch either one before it spreads.

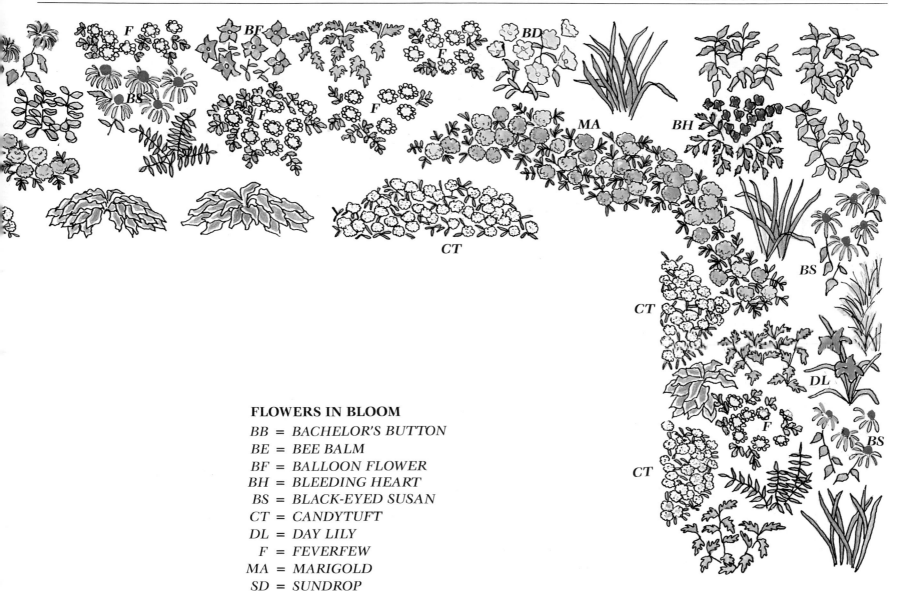

FLOWERS IN BLOOM

BB = BACHELOR'S BUTTON
BE = BEE BALM
BF = BALLOON FLOWER
BH = BLEEDING HEART
BS = BLACK-EYED SUSAN
CT = CANDYTUFT
DL = DAY LILY
 F = FEVERFEW
MA = MARIGOLD
SD = SUNDROP

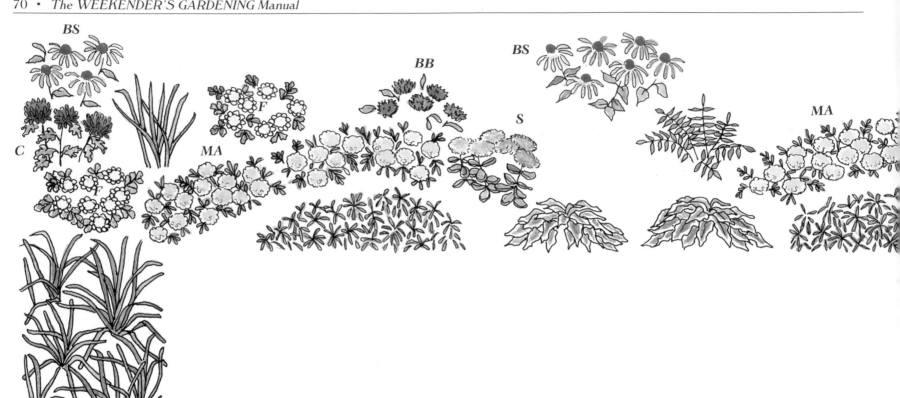

A LARGE INFORMAL GARDEN: FALL

The garden continues to provide viewing pleasure and cut-flower arrangements throughout the fall. While you're looking and cutting, however, you should also be working. This is the time of year for a good garden clean up—remove weeds and faded plants and transplant perennials as needed.

By the time the first snows fall, this garden should look neat and tidy with a stray chrysanthemum or feverfew putting forth a last valiant blossom.

FLOWERS IN BLOOM

BB = *BACHELOR'S BUTTON*
BS = *BLACK-EYED SUSAN*
C = *CHRYSANTHEMUM*
F = *FEVERFEW*
MA = *MARIGOLD*
S = *SEDUM*

Susans, feverfew, and marigolds to encourage a longer bloom period. If you like, cut the bee balm and sundrop to the ground after they have finished blooming to make the garden look neater. This last is not an essential task.

After several years, thinning overgrown clumps of plants will become a major job. You can replant the offshoots to change or expand the design configuration of the garden, give them to your neighbors while perhaps receiving some of their perennials in exchange, or—saddest of all to the maternal sort of gardener—throw the unwanted plants away.

With black-eyed Susans and feverfew scattered throughout, this garden will provide you with touches of yellow and white all summer long. At various stages, reds, pinks, purples, blues, oranges, and lavenders will come and go. For over half a year, the garden will yield an abundant amount of cut flowers. You can fill your home with lovely arrangements for months on end—all for less than two hours work each weekend.

CHAPTER FIVE

A WEEKEND VEGETABLE GARDEN

As any lover of good food knows, there's a world of difference between fresh vegetables and fresh-picked vegetables. Fresh vegetables are the kind that you buy at the produce section of your grocery store, at an outdoor market, or even at a farmer's stand. These vegetables can be quite good and nutritious. Still, they do not compare with those that are fresh-picked from your own garden—vegetables that are harvested a half-hour or less before being eaten.

Taste is the factor that separates fresh from fresh-picked vegetables. It is one of the primary motives for having a home vegetable garden. Garden devotees can easily satisfy their needs through working with flowers, and such a task is also esthetically pleasing. Gourmands, however, can only be appeased with the harvest from their own vegetable gardens. If you are both—a lover of gardening and of fresh food—you should definitely plan to have a weekend vegetable garden. This chapter will tell you how to go about it.

SUN AND SOIL
MEETING TWO SPECIAL REQUIREMENTS

When you look at the harvest schedule at the end of this chapter, you might wonder how you will be able to eat all your fine bounty. This cornucopia is somewhat deceiving, however, because it is very selective. Vegetables are much fussier than flowers, and your options are more limited. You must, for example, have a garden bed that receives a minimum of six hours of full sun each day. The more sun,

Good soil is an important prerequisite for a vegetable garden.

the greater the harvest and the better tasting your vegetables will be. While it is possible to have a shade flower garden, it is not possible to have a shade vegetable garden.

You also must have proper soil. You can't fudge here the way you can in the flower garden. What do you think of when asked to picture good, rich soil? Does fine, warm brown dirt, the kind that separates freely, come to mind? If so, you are on your way to visualizing the type of soil needed for your vegetable garden. That soil must be rich in organic matter and in nutrients. These can come through the addition of manure every spring or through the application of commercial fertilizers. It is also essential that the soil be the teensiest bit on the acidic side. Chapter Two reviews how to test your soil for acidity and how to read the pH scale. The pH reading for your vegetable garden should be around 6.5.

You must enroll your local nursery in your garden plans. In general, vegetable seedlings are not shipped through the mail. You will have to rely on the nursery to provide these for you, as well as for advice on how to make your soil suitable for vegetables and for supplies to enrich the soil and fertilize the vegetables.

VEGETABLES THAT CAN'T BE INCLUDED
DOING WITHOUT

There is a sad fact facing the weekend gardener: It is not possible to grow every kind of vegetable. Root crops, for

Vegetable seedlings are best obtained from your local nursery.

In addition to crunchy stalks, garden celery will provide healthy, tasty green leaves.

After this broccoli head is cut from the plant, smaller side heads will appear.

example, are planted by seed, and the weekend gardener will not be around to give the newly emerging seedlings the daily watering they need. This means—to the joy of a great many children, one supposes—that turnips are out. So too, however, are carrots, beets, and rutabagas.

The weekend gardener also will not be available to tend to the needs of vegetables requiring almost daily harvesting when they are at their peak. This group includes beans of all kinds and peas. Left unharvested, the vegetables on these plants become tough and seedy and stop producing new crops. There will be little for you to eat, and the space these plants take up will be wasted.

It is also assumed that the weekend gardener will not have the time to prepare a large garden bed. This means that vegetables that take up a lot of room, plants such as corn and butternut squash, will not be included in the garden plans.

The last group of vegetables that are denied to the weekend gardener are the members of the squash family. With the exception of butternut squash, these are all prone to a horrible pest known as the squash borer. You can leave your country retreat one weekend with a fond farewell to a healthy, vigorous plant covered with flowers and baby unripened squashes and return the next to a plant that is flat on its back with its fruit all withered. No amount of water will revive it to its former glory. If you were to cut inside the stems, you would find horrible, white wormlike creatures that have literally eaten the heart out of your plant.

With all this denial, is there anything left? Yes, quite a bit, as a matter of fact. The remainder of this chapter describes the workings of a very small vegetable garden that yields enough produce to feed a family of four every weekend throughout the entire summer. In some cases, there will even be enough to share with friends, although the garden is designed to produce vegetables for only the family in order to cut down on the time required for harvesting.

A SUGGESTED PLAN
GROWING YOUR OWN VEGETABLES

The garden in this example is only one hundred feet (thirty meters) square and contains seventeen different vegetables and three herbs. It is suggestive only. Readers will want to modify their gardens to satisfy their own palates.

When it comes to vegetable gardens, small is better as far as work goes. The smaller the garden, the less weeding and the less watering required. Two techniques provide the key to maximizing your yield from a small space. The first technique is known as intensive gardening, the second as double cropping. These are fancy names for very practical approaches.

Intensive gardening means that you plant your vegetables very close together and harvest the younger ones to give the others room to grow. Double cropping means that as soon as you have finished harvesting one vegetable, another is ready to step in line. Both techniques ensure that space is not wasted.

In the illustration for the early summer weekend garden, for example, lettuce seedlings have been packed in be-

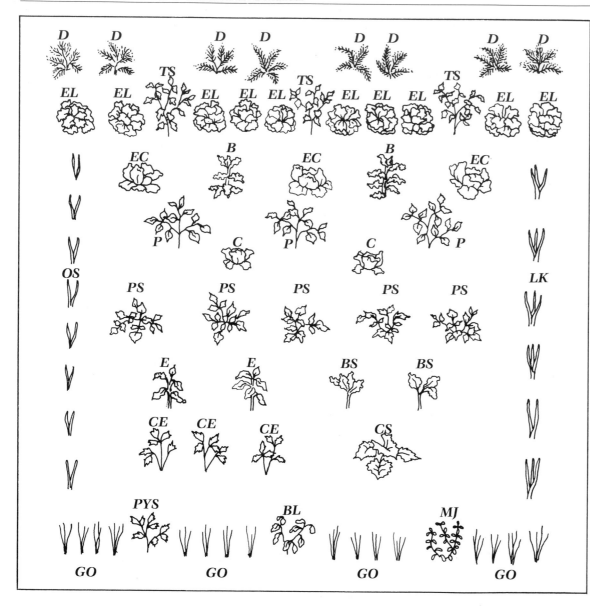

B = *BROCCOLI*
BL = *BASIL*
BS = *BRUSSEL SPROUT*
C = *CAULIFLOWER*
CE = *CELERY*
CS = *CUCUMBER SEEDLING*
D = *DILL*
E = *EGGPLANT*
EC = *EARLY CABBAGE*
EL = *EARLY LETTUCE*
GO = *GREEN ONION*
LK = *LEEKS*
MJ = *MARJORAM*
OS = *ONION SET*
P = *PEPPER*
PS = *POTATO SEEDLING*
PYS = *PARSLEY SEEDLING*
TS = *TOMATO SEEDLING*

By early summer, the suggested vegetable garden should look something like this. There are dill plants along the top edge of the garden, then lettuce and tomato seedlings. Cabbage and broccoli share a row. Then come peppers and two cauliflower plants. Potato plants are shown in the next row. The following two rows consist of eggplant and brussel sprout seedlings, and celery and cucumber seedlings. The left border of the garden is made up of onion sets and the right of leek seeds. Parsley, basil, and marjoram are planted after green onions are pulled.

B = BROCCOLI
BL = BASIL
BS = BRUSSEL SPROUT
CE = CELERY
CT = CHERRY TOMATO
CU = CUCUMBER
E = EGGPLANT
K = KALE
LK = LEEK
LL = LATE LETTUCE
MJ = MARJORAM
P = PEPPER
PO = POTATO
PY = PARSLEY
T = TOMATO

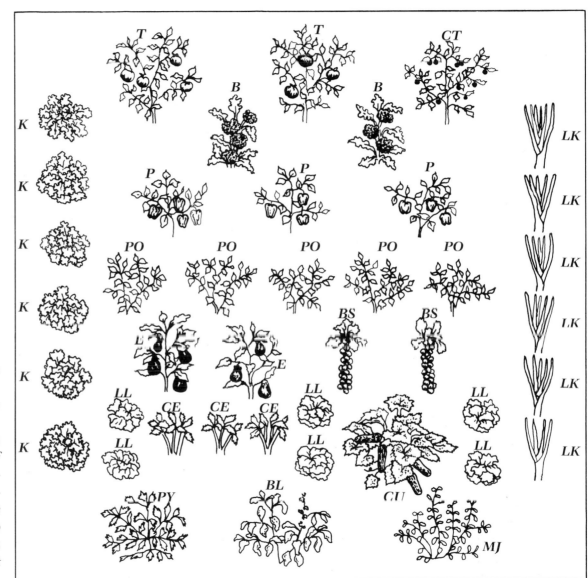

By late summer, the vegetable garden is still very productive. Tomatoes, broccoli, and pepper plants dominate the top third. In the middle, potatoes, eggplants, and brussel sprout plants are ready to be harvested. The bottom part consists of celery, late lettuce plants, and cucumbers, with the parsley, basil, and marjoram along the border. On the left, a line of kale plants await the first frost to enrich their flavor. The row of leeks on the right can be harvested through light frosts and snow.

tween the tomato seedlings. It is assumed that three weeks after being put in the ground, five lettuce plants will be harvested for the weekend salads; by the next weekend, the plants will have grown so that only three will be needed for salads; by the following two weekends, the heads will be so large that one will suffice for two salads. As the lettuce heads are being pulled, the tomato plants are expanding and filling up the space the lettuce vacated. Dill tends to grow faster than tomatoes at the beginning, so these plants are shooting up into the sun for you to use with your spring and early summer vegetables. By the time the tomato plants have overtaken the dill, the dill plants will have gone to seed and be ready to be pulled out of the garden.

The cherry tomato plant should produce at least a hundred tomatoes and you can probably get twenty or more tomatoes from each of the other plants. While you are waiting for the tomatoes to ripen on the vine, pick some of the green ones. Fresh green tomatoes are a delight that cannot be bought in stores. Dice, sprinkle with curry powder, and then simmer them for about five minutes in butter—a quick and easy garnish for a rice dish. When frost seems likely, bring all the green tomatoes in; they will ripen slowly on your kitchen counter during the week.

Three cabbage plants are included in the scheme. Two can probably be used on one weekend and the third on another. Cabbage goes to seed, and most heads, when formed, cannot last longer than two weeks in a garden. As the cabbage plants are harvested, there is room for the broccoli plants to grow and spread their long leaves. After you cut the main broccoli head, little side shoots appear and these can be snipped off all summer.

The wonderful thing about bell peppers is that they can be eaten green or allowed to stay on the plant and ripen into a brilliant red. There is no set harvest period. You pick them when you want them. Within two months of setting out your pepper seedlings, you will have enough peppers to harvest every weekend through frost. There is, however, a caveat to this bold statement. If you live in a climate where the summers are exceptionally hot, the peppers may not start producing until late August or early September. If the temperature does not go down to the low sixties (about fifteen degrees Celsius) at night, the pepper blossoms will fall off in the heat. As soon as things cool down, however, the plants go back in action.

Two cauliflower plants are included in the scheme. They must be picked on successive weekends; otherwise, they will bolt, becoming tough and producing flowers.

After the cauliflower has been harvested, dispose of the plants to make room for the green foliage of the potato plants. When small purple flowers appear at the top of this foliage, nature is signaling that very tiny potatoes are ready to be harvested. It is probably best to wait a weekend or so after that. Then you can begin to harvest as you want. The longer you leave the potatoes in the ground, the bigger they grow. To harvest, just plunge a pitchfork gently into the soil and pull up. Gently shake the dirt loose, and you should see new potatoes left on the tool or visible on top of the dirt pile. Do this several times to make sure you have found all the potatoes.

Peppers are wonderful for the weekend vegetable garden. They can be picked green or allowed to ripen to a sweet red.

Eggplant, like peppers, turns quite productive in cooler summer weather. You can get six or more vegetables from each plant. Brussel sprouts have a long growing season and are not ready to be picked until the end of summer. Many gardeners insist that light frosts improve their flavor.

If you cut just one or two stalks from the outer edge of the celery plants, you should have celery all summer long. The green leaves on top can be trimmed without mercy and add wonderful flavor to soups. Next to the celery can be found several summer lettuce plants. Buy the kind described as "slow to bolt" or "heat resistant" and you should be able to extend your green salad season through mid-summer.

Cucumbers can be risky but are so wonderful on hot summer days that they are included here. This area in the illustration on page 79 indicates a two-foot- (sixty-centimeter-) high garden fence with an approximately two-foot (sixty-centimeter) radius. Just stick the ends of the fence in the ground to anchor it in place. The bush seedlings are planted inside and mulched heavily. Cucumbers need lots of water, and the first task upon arrival for the weekend should be a deep splash of water for them. When in their prime, these plants are wonderfully prolific. You will find that some of the cucumbers will have grown too big and seedy during your five days away from the garden, but there should be at least one or two that will be just perfect for your weekend stay.

In the garden scheme, onion sets are planted in two long rows. The first row is picked as scallions and then replaced in early summer with parsley, basil, and marjoram. This is a bit later than these herbs are usually planted, but they will be at their peak at just the time the tomatoes are being harvested madly. The other onions should be allowed to mature. Pick them as needed, and then pull out the remainder and store in a dry area. In their place, put in a row of kale seedlings. As with brussel sprouts, the flavor of this vegetable is also supposed to improve with frosts. You can even harvest kale through light snows.

The last vegetable in your garden can be found in the row of leeks. These are a terribly expensive delicacy in most stores and are exceptionally easy to grow. They take a long time, but by early fall you should be able to harvest some each weekend. Even when they are at their tiniest seedling stage, you can pull them up and use them to add flavor to bouillon or broth.

ENJOYING THE BOUNTY
A HARVEST SCHEDULE

The following gives you some idea of the produce you can expect from this garden plan during various stages of the growing season.

LATE SPRING, EARLY SUMMER: lettuce, scallions, dill, cabbage, broccoli.

MID-SUMMER: broccoli side shoots, cherry tomatoes, green tomatoes, peppers, cauliflower, celery, onions, eggplant, lettuce.

LATE SUMMER: tomatoes, cherry tomatoes, broccoli side shoots, peppers, potatoes, eggplant, celery, cucumber, onions, parsley, basil, majoram.

EARLY FALL: tomatoes, cherry tomatoes, broccoli side shoots, pepper, potatoes, eggplant, brussel sprouts, celery, parsley, marjoram.

MID-FALL: kale, brussel sprouts, leeks, potatoes, celery, parsley.

LATE FALL: kale, brussel sprouts, leeks, parsley.

WORKING IT OUT
CHORES FOR THE VEGETABLE GARDEN

Now that your appetite has been whetted by the harvest schedule above, it's time to get down to the dirty work. There are six essential tasks associated with a vegetable garden: preparing the soil, planting, staking, mulching, watering, and harvesting.

Keen readers might note that the list does not contain two well-known garden jobs: weeding and controlling diseases and pests. Weeding is easily eliminated through mulching. Control of disease and pests is another matter.

With the exception of rotenone (an insecticide made from the roots of the plant derris), most other poisons require a wait of several days after application before the vegetables can be picked and eaten. A weekend gardener does not have the luxury of such time. Indiscriminate spraying of the garden before leaving on Sunday evening could destroy beneficial as well as harmful insects. The garden described in this chapter is too small to support natural predators such as the ladybug and the praying mantis, that eat other insects. In such a garden, the best approach to take toward disease and pest control happens to be the most drastic: Eliminate the afflicted plant and hope for better luck the following year. A simple tomato worm or two can be squashed easily (albeit messily) on the stem; but if a plant appears to be totally covered with something or is dying in its tracks, send it to your garbage can. As an extra precaution, throw away some of the surrounding dirt, in case eggs or other organisms are getting ready to hatch there.

For many, preparing the soil is one of the dullest and dreariest aspects of weekend gardening. There is no getting away from it, however. If you have the money, perhaps you could hire someone else to do this chore. Basically, as soon as the ground is thawed and dry enough to work with in the spring, the garden must be turned over. This is the best time to work in peat moss, sand, or (if your plants were less than spectacular the year before) fertilizer. Ask your local nursery for advice on what to add to your soil. You also can buy fancy (and rather expensive) kits to test for all sorts of soil nutrients, but if your plants are growing well, such a purchase shouldn't be necessary. If your garden is larger than the one shown in this chapter, you might want to have your soil rototilled (that means a machine does the work for you). For a 100-foot- (thirty-meter-) square garden, however, turning over with a shovel is probably best. Sprinkle on whatever you are adding to the soil and then work it in, much as one folds beaten egg whites in a cake batter. After the ground has been thoroughly dug and turned, rake it smooth.

You are now ready to plant. All seedlings should be put in following the directions given in Chapter Two. In addition,

Tomatoes are the only staked plant in this vegetable garden.

this garden scheme requires the use of onion sets, potato eyes, and leek seeds. Onion sets are baby bulbs and can be bought at your nursery. They are easy to plant. Just make a line with your hoe as deep as the onion set is tall, about one inch (two and a half centimeters) to two inches (five centimeters). Now you're going to practice intensive gardening. Onion sets should be planted about six inches (fifteen centimeters) apart; your spacing will be two inches (five centimeters). You make up for this crowding by thinning; that is, by picking every two young scallions and leaving the third. By the time the remaining onions are full grown, they are six inches (fifteen centimeters) apart.

While potatoes can be bought from a grocery store, quartered, and then planted, you are well advised to buy disease-free seed tubers from your local nursery. To plant, just dig a hole about five inches (thirteen centimeters) deep and drop the tuber in. It's really quite simple. Space the plants so that they are ten inches (twenty-five centimeters) to twelve inches (thirty centimeters) apart. In the garden example here, you should be able to plant about eight tubers—enough to yield at least thirty to forty potatoes.

The leeks are the only plant in this book where you actually use seeds. A member of the onion family, leeks can reseed themselves, so there is really no reason why you shouldn't try seeding them yourself. Buy a seed packet at the store or through the mail and follow the directions. The plants will need to be thinned.

You will only need three stakes for this vegetable garden. Buy them from your local nursery and then save for use each year. Be sure you get the strongest tomato stakes possible (it's worth the initial investment) and put them in

Since leeks will reseed themselves, there is no reason why you can't try growing them from seed in your weekend garden.

the ground *before* planting the tomato seedlings. As the tomatoes grow, gently tie the plants to the stakes to keep them upright. Old rags or old nylon stockings make good ties because they are soft and do not cut into the tomato stems.

Unlike flowers, vegetables do not totally recover from a short-term lack of water. While the plant may look like it feels better, the vegetables themselves will have suffered. This is one reason why mulching is absolutely essential in the vegetable garden: It helps to conserve water. Mulching a plant is somewhat similar to tucking a child in at night. You want to put enough material around the plant to keep it healthy but not too much to suffocate it. The further you get from the plant, however, the more you put on because mulch does throttle weeds. Mulches were discussed in greater detail in Chapter Two.

The older your plants become, the more time you will spend watering them. Vegetables must have a deep watering; that means enough water to soak in, at least two inches (five centimeters) to three inches (seven and a half centi-

meters) deep. If you aren't sure the plants have had enough, dig a hole nearby and see how dry the dirt is underneath.

Harvesting is included as a chore rather than a reward in this discussion because, if you don't do it faithfully for some of the vegetables, they may well stop producing for you. It is also important to pull up plants (such as the cabbage, cauliflower, and dill plants) once they no longer bear vegetables so that there will be room for other plants to grow. This also helps to keep your garden neat and tidy, a situation that deters unwanted pests and diseases. Be sure to pull up and clear all vegetables from the garden by winter.

This list of chores may seem long and onerous, but remember that they are spread out over more than six months. True to the premise of this book, you will spend no more than two hours, and often considerably less time, in your vegetable garden each weekend. In return, you will be enjoying the wonderful taste of fresh-picked vegetables and the pleasure of knowing that you grew them yourself.

CHAPTER SIX

NECESSITIES AND NATURAL DISASTERS

Into every gardener's life a little sadness will fall; this chapter tells you how to minimize it in some cases and accept it in others. Many of the points covered here have been woven throughout the text. Nevertheless, they all deserve separate coverage in their own right.

YOUR LOCAL NURSERY
ENSURING YOUR GARDEN'S HAPPINESS

Time and time again, throughout this book, reference has been made to your local nursery. It's just about impossible to have a weekend garden without one. The people at the nursery are the ones who will comfort you in your sorrow, advise you in your ignorance, and join you to celebrate your successes; they are indispensable. If your nursery is not helpful, it should not be in business; look for another one. Find one to whom you can take your soil, your diseased leaves, your stunted flowers yearning to be lovely. They will recommend, admittedly at a price, the remedies you should take.

Your local nursery is also a good source of seedlings. It's really best to plant flowers on the day you buy them. If you order by mail, the plants may not arrive on a day you can put them in the ground. In addition, the nursery will supply you with soil-testing kits, mulches, and any tools that you may need.

Remember, you do not have the time to be an expert gardener; your local nursery makes a living by providing such expertise.

NINE ESSENTIAL GARDEN TOOLS
DIGGING IN

There are all sorts of wonderful gadgets that are great fun to play with in your garden. Ask yourself, however: Do I really need them? Do I want to spend the money in the first place and the time cleaning, maintaining, and storing them in the second place? If your answer is no to either question, forget the fancy tools and concentrate on the following basics.

TWO TROWELS. Get a fat one and a thin one. The former is recommended for planting and transplanting deep-rooted perennials; the latter is especially suited for planting small seedlings.

ONE BULBER. This is a handy little tool for planting bulbs of all sorts. Make sure it comes with measurements on its side so that you know exactly how far down you are digging (different bulbs have different depth requirements).

ONE DIGGING SPADE. This is handy for digging up larger clumps of the garden, for working in peat moss or lime, and for planting large, potted flowers.

ONE HOSE. Measure the distance from the spigot to the garden to determine the length of hose you will need. Generally, those that are five-eighths of an inch (one and a half centimeters) in diameter are best for gardens. Unless you have a very large garden, you will not need a sprinkler system. Just turn the water on gently and hold the hose a

A good, reliable nursery is a necessity for the weekend gardener. It will provide plants, tools, and professional advice.

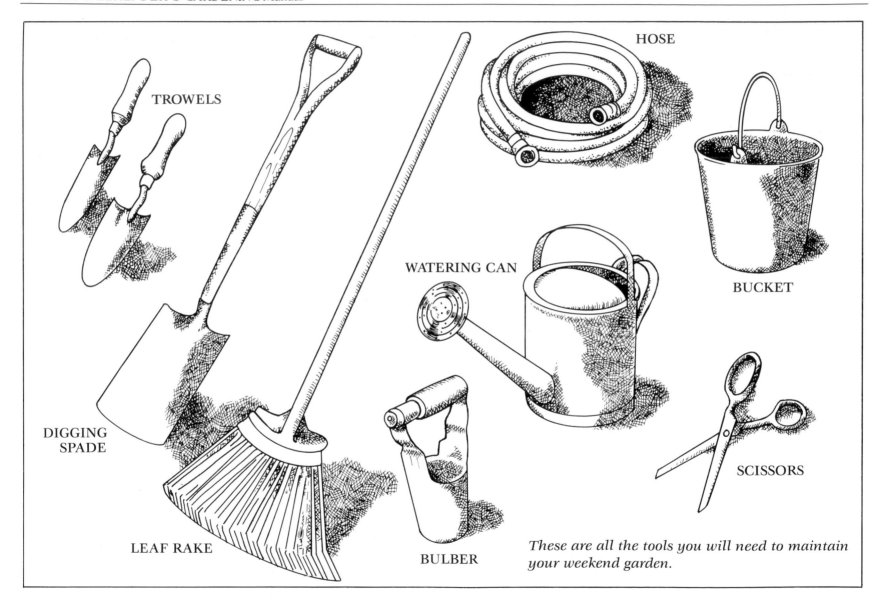

TROWELS

HOSE

DIGGING
SPADE

WATERING CAN

BUCKET

LEAF RAKE

BULBER

SCISSORS

These are all the tools you will need to maintain your weekend garden.

minute or two by each plant so that it will get a good soaking.

ONE WATERING CAN. This is especially good for new seedlings and for smaller plants that will be bowled over by the stream of water coming from a hose. You can buy plastic or metal cans. The metal ones last longer but are heavier to carry. Buy whatever suits you best.

ONE BUCKET. This can be the little plastic kind that children take to the beach to make sand castles. It is helpful for mixing in fertilizer or sand or peat moss when you are planting bulbs or new seedlings.

ONE PAIR OF SCISSORS. These can be the ordinary kind that are used for cutting paper. Set them aside just for garden use. You will need them for cutting flowers and for snipping off seed heads.

ONE LARGE AND ONE SMALL LEAF RAKE. The leaf rake is a must in the spring and fall when you are clearing debris from your garden. Generally, you can use the larger one in the fall because the plants have been knocked out by frost. In the spring, however, when tender perennial shoots are coming, the smaller size (also known as a child's size) is better because you have to lean closer to the ground to see what you are raking over.

These tools take up a minimum amount of space. With the exception of the hose, all should be kept protected from the weather during the growing season. They require little or no maintenance (perhaps a yearly cleaning), do not require a large cash outlay, and will take up very little of your weekend time.

TRYING THE ORGANIC WAY
IT'S HEALTHY, BUT IT'S NOT PERFECT

The organic method of gardening often refers to gardening without the use of poisons. Rachel Carson's *Silent Spring* alerted the world to the terrible consequences of indiscriminate poisoning and since then the nonpoison approach has gained in respectability.

It is important to remember, however, that predators and disease exist to keep plants in a natural balance. In other words, nature wants pests in your garden, and it is often difficult to enlist her as an ally. If you decide to forgo poisons, you must be prepared for a less-than-perfect garden. You can have a pretty garden, but not a perfect one. The following are some tips to help you make it almost perfect.

Keep your garden clean and uncluttered. Make sure there's lots of air circulation around the leaves and stems of your plants. That kind of condition deters the growth of fungi such as mildew. It also allows you to spot and correct insect manifestations before they inundate your garden.

Be prepared to sacrifice one sick plant for the general health of all. If you find a flower covered with insects, cut it off and dispose of it immediately. Similarly, if you find a clump of plants infested with an insect, dig up the clump and throw it away. That deprives these pests of a home base from which to attack the rest of your garden.

If, however, you find only a couple of aphids or spider mties or any other small, ugly-looking creatures feasting on your flowers, try hosing them off with a strong water spray

Weekend gardeners, especially brand new ones, do not have time to become experts in diagnosing plant illnesses. Just take a sample of any sick leaves you might have, and bring them in a plastic bag to your local nursery for advice on how to cure your garden disaster.

(do be careful, in your zeal to knock off pests, that you do not also knock off the plant). If that doesn't seem to work, try a commercial soap spray. These do not contain toxic poisons and can be bought at your nursery.

Other organic gardeners have come up with weird concoctions for sprays. These include mixing hot pepper sauce, garlic, and even ground slugs—a rather offensive lot to put into your blender; this approach, however, does have the virtues of being safe and inexpensive.

Chances are your garden will not be large enough for natural predators, such as ladybugs and praying mantises, to survive. Ladybugs just gobble up aphids, but will you have enough plants to supply an adequate aphid diet for the ladybugs? If not, forget this approach.

Smother weeds with mulch and get down on your hands and knees to dig up the rest. Both these points were covered in Chapter Two. It's important to put your garden in perspective. All gardens—even the world-reknowned Longwood Gardens in Pennsylvania—have weeds. As a weekend gardener, your job will be to keep them from overrunning your gardening, not to obliterate them entirely. Mulching and a good fall cleanup should do the trick.

Know your enemy. Slugs and Japanese beetles leave telltale signs that you can discover during spring planting. Slug eggs look like tiny glass marbles. One slug can deposit over one hundred eggs, usually in a mass. Whenever you come across some, dig them up and throw them away. Japanese beetle grubs are also easily recognizable. If you're the strong, tough sort, just squeeze them between your fingers whenever you inadvertently dig one up. Otherwise, have a garbage bag nearby and throw them in there.

USING HERBICIDES, FUNGICIDES, AND INSECTICIDES

SOME WORDS OF CAUTION

Sometimes, even with the best of intentions on your part, the garden gets blasted by a fungus or a particularly insidious insect. Under ideal conditions, for example, one scientist has calculated that a pair of cabbage aphids could produce enough descendants to outweigh the population of the earth in just one growing season! When your garden looks like it is going to be outweighed by pests, it is time for an important decision: Should you or shouldn't you use poison?

Remember, poison kills. Just read the instructions on some of the bottles: You have to wear gloves, warn your neighbors to keep their pets indoors, keep your children away, and dispose of the container without washing it. These are heavy-duty chemicals. Even the makers of these products caution you to work your way up; that is, to start with milder ones before using stronger versions. It is particularly important in this area to rely on the advice of your local nursery.

There are three broad categories of poisons: herbicides, which are used to control weeds; fungicides, which deter the growth of fungi; and insecticides, which kill insects.

Herbicides are generally used at one of two stages of weed growth. Preemergent herbicides kill seeds before they sprout and postemergent herbicides kill the growing plant. Herbicides tend not to be that fastidious. While killing

Slug damage can be lessened by eliminating the eggs. These look like tiny, clear glass marbles and are usually found in groups of one hundred or more. If you find one or two in the soil, dig around the area to see if you can find more. Throw each and every one away.

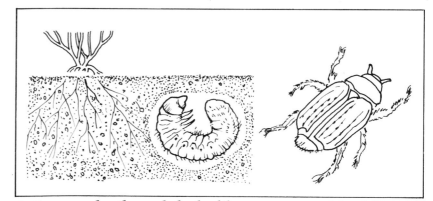

A Japanese beetle grub looks like a creamy, white "C" with tiny hairs. You will often find them when preparing your soil or transplanting seedlings. If you're cold hearted, just squeeze them between your fingers. More genteel individuals will prefer to dump grubs into a nearby trash bag.

weeds, many will also do away with other, more valuable, plants. Unless you have a very large garden, there should be little reason for you to use herbicides. Good use of mulch, some judicious hand weedings, and a fall cleanup should solve all weed problems for the weekend gardener.

Fungicides are chemical formulations that are used either as preventive measures by establishing an environment hostile to fungi or as an active agent by eliminating established infections. There are dozens of fungicides, each with specific applications. Many plants are almost immune to fungi infections and, if you choose your flowers carefully, you should have little trouble with fungi. In any case, do not use a fungicide until you have an actual outbreak. Destroy the infected plants and then use an appropriate preventive fungicide the following year. Be sure to show samples of the sick plants to your local nursery so that you will know which fungicide to buy the next year.

There are few preventive insecticides. Most kill insects that are present in the garden. Here again, it is important to take specimens of infected plants (better yet, of the insects themselves) to your local nursery to have the insect, and thus the appropriate insecticide, identified.

Following are several groups of insecticides the weekend gardener will come across and find useful and effective:

1. BOTANICAL INSECTICIDES. These are made from plant extracts and, in general, are considered among the safest to use. They are particularly appropriate for use on vegetables and fruits because their toxic qualities, as far as humans are concerned, quickly disappear.

2. MICROBIAL INSECTICIDES. These contain the spores of bacteria that kill specific insects. Milky spore disease, which kills Japanese beetle grubs, is probably the most well-known of this group.

3. POISON BAITS. These serve as the "rat traps" of the garden. There are specific baits for specific pests. If there are very young children or pets, like cats or dogs, about, caution is often required in the use of this method of pest control.

4. CHEMICAL INSECTICIDES. This wide group kills insects (and, unfortunately, other forms of life, in many cases) in several ways: immediately through direct contact, slowly through paralysis of the nervous system, and indirectly through ingestion of plant life (the latter are known as systemics—the plant survives but those eating it die). Some chemical insecticides like carbaryl (known widely as Sevin in the United States) are relatively safe and can even be used on vegetables. Others, like DDT, have been proved to be so lethal that their use is either banned or severely restricted in the United States and elsewhere.

Controlling pests and disease takes time, a missing ingredient in the life of a weekend gardener. Perhaps your best approach to this problem is to use plants that are basically healthy as well as strong enough to resist insects. Most of the plants in Appendix A have been chosen with these qualities in mind. By limiting yourself to selections from that list, you should also be restricting your worries about fungi and insects.

CHAPTER SEVEN

A FINAL PEP TALK

Even if you've just skimmed through this book, you should realize by now that gardening is not a scary subject with impossible terminology and exotic rituals. Rather, it's a personal activity: You make of it what you will. There is, after all, no such thing as a perfect garden. Do what suits you best; that's what counts.

There are a few very basic guidelines that this book has emphasized. The first is that the smaller the garden is, the smaller the amount of work required. If you don't want to spend even two hours a weekend in the garden, make sure you have a tiny plot. As shown in Chapter Four, Alan Goodheart had a beautiful, but small, formal summer garden with only one weekend of planting and work.

A second point worth remembering is that the expectation of what your garden can look like is often half the fun—and the source of most of your disappointment. Be prepared for failure. When blight or drought or who knows what other calamity strikes, try to remember Shakespeare's admonition that, "Oft expectation fails, and most oft there where most it promises."

This leads to the third and last observation: Gardening requires patience. Great gardens are not built in a year. The truly magnificent ones found on large British estates are never-ending. Even if you don't aspire to an estate garden, you will find a degree of the same patience necessary. While you can have an instant annual garden, this is not the case with perennials. These take time to spread and to

Gardening with perennials requires patience. Once they have had a chance to settle in and adapt to your garden, however, the results can be spectacular.

make themselves at home. Often, after a weekend of planting in spring, it is disappointing to look at the meager results. Give the plants a chance! A month or so later, they will have settled in and will reward you with growth and a profusion of flowers.

The only hard and fast design rule espoused in this book is: tall plants in the back, short ones up front. It is so easy for the novice gardener to be attracted by a plant's foliage and flowers and to totally neglect its eventual height. Before buying, say to yourself three times: "Ask about its height. Ask about its height. Ask about its height."

The best way to start a weekend garden is to choose easy-to-grow plants. A list is provided for you in Appendix A. Each plant description includes height, bloom period, and color. In general, annuals bloom all summer long and will give you weekend after weekend of colorful display. Perennial plants, on the other hand, provide a greater variety in your garden but, since they do not bloom continuously, you will have to be prepared for some dull garden spots during the growing season. Chapter Four provides examples of gardens with annuals and gardens with perennials.

When trouble comes in the form of insect pests, fungi, or disease, call your local nursery. For all practical purposes,

One design rule that beginning gardeners continually forget is that tall flowers go in the back, short ones up front. Be sure to check the anticipated height of each seedling before planting.

you can't have a weekend garden without such help. Chapters Two and Six review some simple maintenance steps to take so that your calls on the local nursery will be reduced to a minimum.

Money makes a difference. If you have a bundle to spend, use some of it to have your soil professionally prepared. You will find this makes it a lot easier to have a flower garden. If cash does not flow freely through your life, be consoled that most of the plants in Appendix A will do quite well without any special soil preparation. While no one plant is that expensive, by the time you have bought several dozen, you will find the bill can be surprisingly high. If you are on a limited budget, buy perennials that spread—and then try to trade the offspring with neighbors and friends. A good, hearty perennial plant is probably one of your best garden investments.

Perhaps the most important point of all is that gardening is fun. It is rewarding to design and raise a living picture of color. Working with the soil and with varied plant forms gives one a great appreciation of the diversity of life and the wonder of creation. Your weekend gardening moments will be a quiet, refreshing break from the hustle and bustle of the week. Enjoy them and have fun.

A good, sturdy perennial plant is one of the best investments a weekend gardener can make. Black-eyed Susans should be high on your list of easy-to-grow flowers for your garden.

APPENDIX A

PLANTS YOU DEFINITELY WANT TO CONSIDER

Once you have started your weekend garden, you will quickly realize that gardening is an intensely personal activity. It represents a conjunction of your psyche and nature's bounty and quirks. The resulting possibilities are almost endless.

The following plants have been carefully chosen for both attractiveness and sturdiness. All are grown in the author's garden, and every one is recommended as a low-maintenance plant by at least one other gardening expert.

All of these plants should do well in your garden and should give you pleasure. The key word, of course, is *should:* One or two may decide they do not like your garden. That's just the way life—and gardening—works sometimes. Remembering the old adage that there is safety in numbers, it would be best to pick at least ten plants to start with for an enjoyable weekend garden.

HELPFUL FEATURES

There are three aspects of the following list that should prove useful to weekend gardeners.

First, as mentioned in the Preface, the plants are listed by their popular names first and their botanical names second. Some plants, such as ageratum, have a popular name that is their botanical name. Wouldn't it be nice if all plants were like this?

Second, you do not have to look up hardiness zones for any of the perennials. All will grow in areas where the temperatures drop as low as minus twenty degrees (minus twenty-eight degrees Celsius). This temperature range covers the coastal areas of Canada, all of the United Kingdom, and three-fourths of the United States.

Third, you do not have to go on an extensive search to locate these plants. You should be able to find the annuals at your local nursery. If not, ask if they will order them for you or why they do not carry them (they may not be suited for your area). The perennials on the list can be ordered from at least one of the following five firms: Bluestone Perennials, W. Atlee Burpee Seed Co., Spring Hill Nurseries, The Wayside Gardens Co., and White Flower Farm. The addresses for these firms are listed in Appendix D, which also includes many other excellent nurseries that ship plants by mail.

AGERATUM
ANNUAL

This has a lovely, feathery blue flower that blooms on plants often no more than one foot (thirty centimeters) high. Because it is so compact and so covered with flowers, ageratum is widely used in formal gardens. It will bloom all summer long and is very easy to care for—just water weekly and cut off spent blooms when they appear unsightly.

ASTILBE
PERENNIAL

Once a popular plant at Easter time, it somehow fell out of favor but has recently been undergoing a marked revival in popularity. A native of eastern Asia, astilbe is an elegant addition to any garden. It bears lovely twelve-inch- (thirty-centimeter-) to eighteen-inch- (forty-five-centimeter-) high spikes of feathery pink, white, or red flowers in early summer. Astilbe requires a moist soil; its colors will be richer if it is grown in partial shade. The clumps spread slowly and need to be divided about every three years—about the right pace for a weekend gardener.

BACHELOR'S BUTTON, MOUNTAIN BLUET, CORNFLOWER
(Centaurea montana)
PERENNIAL

This sturdy cousin of the annual bachelor's button has a silvery green foliage and large but delicate blue flowers on two-foot- (sixty-centimeter-) high stems. Put them in a sunny location, or even partial shade, and water weekly. That's all you need to do to have these flowers bloom through the summer.

BALLOON FLOWER
(Platycodon grandiflorus)
PERENNIAL

Before opening, the blossoms on this plant resemble small, puffed-up balloons, hence its popular name. After opening, the flowers are star-shaped and usually blue, although one can find pink and white varieties. They appear on stems as tall as three feet (ninety centimeters); fortunately, most do not flop. These plants have no major insect or disease problems and do well in hot, dry locations (you should water on weekends, however). If you feel energetic enough to pick off the dead blooms, you might find these plants blooming almost all summer long. The internationally respected horticulturist Donald Wyman says that these are one of the best of all perennial garden flowers.

BEE BALM, BERGAMOT, OSWEGO TEA
(Monarda didyma)
PERENNIAL

This native American plant is a member of the mint family, which means it spreads easily. As its popular name testifies, it attracts bees. Hummingbirds are also supposed to like this plant. Bee balm grows about three feet (ninety centimeters) tall and bears exotic flowers in purple, red, or pink colors at the height of summer. These are striking in cut-flower arrangements and add brilliant dashes of color to the garden. Bee balm needs little care and will grow in sun or partial shade; full sun keeps it from spreading too quickly.

BEGONIA

ANNUAL

There are two kinds of begonias that appear in gardens: wax, or fibrous-rooted, begonias and tuberous-rooted begonias. The latter bear large, elegant flowers that need to be staked because they are so heavy. Wax begonias are the shorter, old-fashioned variety, and these should fit nicely in a weekend garden. They come in shades of white through red and do best in partial shade. Begonias just bloom and bloom all summer and are a favorite in formal gardens.

BISHOP'S HAT, BARRENWORT

(Epimedium grandiflorum)

PERENNIAL

Most gardeners grow these plants for their foliage: In the spring, the green heart-shaped leaves are tinged with pink; in the fall, they turn an attractive bronze red. You might like them because they are so easy to grow and because they have delicate pink-and-white flowers in the spring. The plants grow only nine inches (twenty-two centimeters) to twelve inches (thirty centimeters) high and are very neat. They do especially well in shade and at the base of trees.

BLEEDING HEART
(Dicentra eximia)
PERENNIAL

This is a classic example of how important it is to know the botanical name of the plant that you want. There are two very popular bleeding hearts. One, *Dicentra spectabilis*, is quite aristocratic and elegant and has true heart-shaped blossoms. Once it stops blooming, however, the foliage tends to die down and leave a rather bare spot in the garden. *Dicentra eximia*, or fern bleeding heart, has flowers that more closely resemble thick pink tears. This species is more suitable for the weekend garden because it can bloom longer (all summer if you feel ambitious enough to water every weekend) and because even without blooming, its dainty, eighteen inch high (forty-five-centimeter-) fernlike foliage is attractive in the garden and in flower arrangements.

BLACK-EYED SUSAN
(*Rudbeckia fulgida*, var. *sullivantii* 'Goldsturm')
PERENNIAL

There are several plants called black-eyed Susan and even several varieties of *Rudbeckia,* one of which is an annual—often called gloriosa daisy—that self-seeds prodigiously. This last can be rather messy. The weekend gardener would be well advised to stick to the neat and tidy perennial version named here; it has been described as representing the black-eyed Susan to perfection. It grows in large clumps that are two-and-a-half feet (seventy-six centimeters) high and should be divided every four or five years (a not very arduous task). It bears lots of yellow flowers with dark centers from mid-summer right through the first frost or two.

BROWALLIA
ANNUAL

If you have a shady spot, this could be the plant for you. Bearing dark blue colors, browallia has been described as a low-growing jewel that glistens throughout the summer. It needs moist soil, but most shady spots naturally fit that description. This plant is also good for pots and hanging baskets.

BUGLOSS, DWARF ANCHUSA
(*Brunnera macrophylla*)
PERENNIAL

This plant sends forth blue flowers that very much resemble forget-me-nots in the spring and then forms a very attractive mound of dark green, heart-shaped leaves. The leaves grow quite large, and the mounds can be as tall as eighteen inches (forty-five-centimeters). Bugloss is easy to grow if given light shade and a somewhat moist soil.

CANDYTUFT
(Iberis sempervirens)
PERENNIAL

These tough little evergreen plants, covered with white flowers in late spring and often again in the fall, thrive in full sun and will also perform for you in partial shade. They are wonderful along the border as they grow only four inches (ten centimeters) to nine inches (twenty-two centimeters) high. You can forget all about them as far as weekly care is concerned and just enjoy them for their attractiveness.

CARPET BUGLE, BUGLEWEED
(Ajuga reptans)
PERENNIAL

This hardy plant lives up to its name: Give it a year or two, and you will find a carpet of shiny, dark green leaves covering the garden area where it is planted. Weeds rarely have room to break through. In the spring, these plants present an added bonus: Blue-flowered spikes between four inches (ten centimeters) and six inches (fifteen centimeters) high appear in profusion. But be careful. Carpet bugle is a member of the prolific mint family and often spreads into areas where it is not wanted.

CHIVES
(Allium schoenoprasum)
PERENNIAL

These are a great bonus to the garden because they are edible as well as attractive and are just about immune to any pest or disease. Members of the hardy onion family, chive plants are covered in spring with small round heads of tiny lavender flowers about ten inches (twenty-five centimeters) high. They are a nice addition to floral arrangements. Throughout the summer months, the plants are innocuous occupants of the garden (often tucked away in the back) and can be cut every weekend for flavoring soups and salads. It appears that the more you cut them, the more they grow. Occasionally, they will even reward you with a blossom or two in the fall.

CELOSIA
ANNUAL

In England, this is sometimes known as Prince of Wales Feathers, which is as good a description as any of this regal, plumed flower. The bright red species is known as cockscomb and is an old-fashioned favorite. Today's breeders have developed plants that range in height from one foot (thirty centimeters) to four feet (120 centimeters) and in color from red to purple to gold. Celosia is particularly effective in the back of a sunny garden and can grow quite well with only a weekly watering.

CHRYSANTHEMUM
PERENNIAL
The origins of this popular fall flower are lost in ancient history. Confucius wrote about its blooms almost twenty-five hundred years ago. It has long been honored in Japan, where September Ninth is an official holiday in honor of chrysanthemums, and the flowers are exhibited throughout the fall in temples and shrines as well as in public gardens. In the U.S., the Botanic Garden Conservatory at the foot of the nation's Capitol building sets aside the month of November for a spectacular chrysanthemum display. Thanks to the efforts of horticulturalists throughout the world, particularly in England and Australia, the chrysanthemum now comes in all sizes, shapes, and colors. The weekend gardener should check with a local nursery to find which ones are best.

COLEUS
ANNUAL
Grown for its multicolored leaves, this plant is often found in pots indoors as well as in gardens outdoors. You will have to pinch off the nondescript purple flowers to keep the plant from becoming leggy, but that should take no more than three or four minutes on a weekend. Coleus grows well in sun or shade. However, because it does need moist soil, it should probably be planted in the shade for a weekend garden.

COLUMBINE
(Aquilegia)
PERENNIAL

The state flower of Colorado, this attractive plant bears exotically shaped flowers that are white on the inside and colored on the outside. The colors vary from palest pink to darkest purple; yellow columbines are rather rare. The flowers appear on the end of very thin stems that rise one foot (thirty centimeters) to three feet (ninety centimeters) above its foliage. These never flop and, when blooming in late spring, add a lovely accent to the garden. If you let the plants go to seed, you can just shake the pods anywhere you like, and the next year you will have columbine growing where the seeds landed. The foliage is often disfigured by an insect called leaf miner; this problem can be easily solved by simply pulling up the plants after they have gone to seed.

CORAL BELLS
(Heuchera sanguinea)
PERENNIAL

This is a wonderful addition to any garden, but particularly to a weekend one. You just plant it and forget about it. Compact clumps—about twelve inches (thirty centimeters) high—of green leaves will grow throughout the year. In the summer, slender stems about two feet (sixty centimeters) high will appear. Each tip will carry groups of tiny, delicate, bell-shaped flowers that look grand in floral arrangements. The most common variety has a coral pink flower; fancier gardeners now include red and white flowered plants in their beds.

COREOPSIS
(C. lanceolata)
PERENNIAL

This is a perfect plant for a weekend garden: It comes up year after year; is slow to spread; bears bright, yellow, daisylike blooms on two-foot- (thirty-centimeter-) high stems all summer; and needs only full sun, a weekly watering, and a plucking of faded flowers to prolong the bloom period. Little wonder that this plant has been called the workhorse of the garden.

CROCUS
PERENNIAL

Even people who don't consider themselves gardeners have crocus flowers scattered throughout their property. Only three inches (seven and a half centimeters) to six inches (fifteen centimeters) high, their brilliant purple, white, and gold blossoms herald the splendors of spring to come. Once planted, nature takes over and the crocus will not only divide but also reseed itself. Not all crocus are hardy to minus twenty degrees (minus twenty-eight degrees Celsius). Two that do meet this specification are *C. susianus,* a yellow or dark orange crocus originating in the Crimea, and *C. vernus,* a European native that is the most widely grown crocus in the U.S.

DAFFODIL
(Narcissus)
PERENNIAL

Not even the *Oxford Dictionary of English Etymology* is quite sure how the term daffodil crept into our language. Sixty years ago, the British garden writer E. T. Ellis said that daffodil was the English version and *narcissus* the Latin version of the same family of plants. Since then, the use of the Latin name has triumphed, at least in the U.S. Donald Wyman, horticulturalist emeritus of the Arnold Arboretum of Harvard University, says that daffodil is the popular name for only some members of the *narcissus* family. And, in case you are wondering about the plural form of the last, the American Daffodil Society has declared that the word is the same in both the plural and the singular. Not all gardeners follow this dictate, and occasionally one comes across the word *Narcissi*. Linguistics aside, these are extremely easy to care for. Buy several kinds with different blooming periods so that you can enjoy them all spring long.

DAY LILY
(Hemerocallis)
PERENNIAL

The botanical name for this plant comes from the Greek and means, "beautiful for a day." Borne on long stalks called scapes, hybrid day lilies have as many as fifty buds—each blooming one or two at a time. If there is space, clumps of day lilies are perfect for the weekend gardener. They will bloom over a three-to-four-week period, have no serious pest problems, need watering only in prolonged dry spells, grow in sun or partial shade, and need to be divided only every six or seven years—at most. There are thousands of cultivars. Their heights range from one foot (thirty centimeters) to seven feet (213 centimeters), their shapes from bells to circles, their colors from all reds to all yellows, and their bloom periods from early to middle to late summer. Your most difficult task with these plants will be deciding which ones are best for your garden.

DUSTY MILLER, SILVER GROUNDSEL
(Senecio cineraria)
PERENNIAL, BUT TREATED AS AN ANNUAL IN COLDER CLIMATES

One of at least five plants that go by the name of dusty miller, *senecio cineraria* is grown primarily for its lovely foliage. This is lacelike and silvery gray, and adds a striking accent to any garden. In order to keep the plants from becoming leggy and messy, the leaves should be periodically snipped—an easy chore on the weekend. Dusty miller needs only occasional watering and grows best in sun, although you can plant it in partial shade.

FERNS
PERENNIAL

These followed the algae and mosses in the evolution of plants on earth and can now be found from the tropics to the Arctic. This hardiness and variety is amazing in a plant that appears so fine and delicate. Thoreau said, "Nature made ferns for pure leaves." The beauty of their form and the range of subtle greens make these an attractive addition in gardens as well as in flower arrangements. If you have a moist and, preferably, partially shady spot, try some ferns. Look about in nearby woods or in neighbors' gardens to see what kinds will do best in your area.

FEVERFEW
(Chrysanthemum parthenium or *Matricaria parthenium)*
PERENNIAL

This is one of the plants the Pilgrims brought to Plymouth, and it's easy to understand why. Covered with small daisylike flowers and loaded with green, feathery foliage, this one-foot- (thirty-centimeter-) to two-foot- (sixty-centimeter-) high plant just takes off, spreading throughout the garden and blooming from early summer through several frosts. The Pilgrims used it in medicines for fever (hence its name), and it is supposed to act as an insect repellent when diluted with water and splashed on skin. Today, the old-fashioned variety is viewed by many as a weed and is rarely found in catalogs. The double variety, called snowball feverfew, is a much more refined version and probably more proper for a weekend gardener who does not want to spend time pulling out unwanted seedlings.

GERANIUM
(Pelargonium hortorum)
ANNUAL

There are many plants that go by the name geranium. Some are perennial, some are like vines, and some bloom in the woodlands in early spring. This one is the popular house geranium that grows one foot (thirty centimeters) to two feet (sixty centimeters) high. You can plant it indoors, in pots or tubs on a patio, or in any sunny spot with good soil in your garden. It is an especially popular summer flower because its colors are so pretty—all sorts of whites, pinks, and reds—and because of the length of its bloom. Geraniums should be watered every week, and faded flowers should be snipped.

GRAPE HYACINTHS
(Muscari botryoides)
PERENNIAL
This is an early flowering bulb that adds a touch of blue to the spring garden. The flowers are small racemes at the end of spikes no more than one foot (thirty centimeters) tall. Plant them in the fall; they will need no care and will increase naturally. What more could a weekend gardener require?

HEN AND CHICKENS
(Sempervivum tectorum)
PERENNIAL
This is another one of the plants brought to the New World by the first colonists. In those days, it had a utilitarian function—the plants were used for binding soil on the sod roofs of cottages (*tectorum* is Latin for "roof"). Today, it is a low-growing succulent that is pleasing in appearance and undemanding in manner.

The low, green leaves are shaped like roses and little baby offshoots sprout from the side (the mother plant looks like a hen with chicks peeping out from under her). It grows in partial shade but does best in sun. If you like, you can dig up some in the fall and use them as houseplants during the winter.

HOSTA
PERENNIAL

Sometimes called funkia or plantain lily, these ornamental plants are often seen in long borders surrounding houses, driveways, or shady parts of property. They are a lazy gardener's delight: a handsome, symmetrical mound of heart-shaped leaves that send forth purple or white flowers. There are many species, with leaf sizes ranging from three inches (seven and a half centimeters) to fifteen inches (thirty-eight centimeters). The larger ones produce clumps almost five feet (152 centimeters) across—be sure to give them adequate space if you include them in your garden. The leaves come in many shades of green, and some are white and green. Hostas require little work and only ask that there be some organic matter in the soil where they are planted. This is a favorite shade garden plant.

IMPATIENS
ANNUAL

An ambitious breeding program has made this a perfect flower for the shade garden. The height of today's plants vary from six inches (fifteen centimeters) to thirty inches (seventy-six centimeters), and there is a wide range of colors from white through red. Impatiens bloom away all summer long. Make sure you water them every weekend, and then just sit back and enjoy them. Often they reseed themselves, so you don't even have to go through the bother of replanting them the following year.

IRIS
PERENNIAL

There are more than 150 species of iris spread throughout the northern temperate zone. One of the most handsome is known as the pogon or bearded species. These are not for a weekend garden, beautiful though they may be. These irises are constantly attacked by a dreadful pest known as iris borer; it literally bores its way down the leaves and then through the iris rhizome. After this devastation, the iris plants generally succumb to a particularly bad-smelling disease known as soft rot. The weekend gardener must be content with the apogon or beardless species, which is quite lovely in its own right. The Siberian iris *(I. siberica)* is an excellent easy-care variety. The plants grow about three feet (ninety centimeters) tall and their flowers, which bloom in late spring, come in shades of blue and pink. While these irises prefer a home near water, they are gracious (and tough) enough to survive drought, and their long, graceful foliage remains a handsome addition to the garden long after the flowers have faded.

JACOB'S LADDER
(Polemonium caeruleum)
PERENNIAL

This has been described as an ideal plant for a beginning gardener. Just plunk it in average soil, make sure it has at least some sun during the day, and water it on weekends. You will find yourself with a plant that has low, deep-green, fernlike foliage and that bears lovely, delicate blue flowers on one-and-a-half-foot (forty-five-centimeter) stems in late spring. The flowers are quite lovely and long-lasting in arrangements. The foliage is attractive in the garden even when the flowers stop blooming.

MARIGOLD
(Tagetes)
ANNUAL

Marigolds originated in South America and were discovered growing wild in Mexico by Cortez. He took seeds back to Spain, and the flowers of the new plant were placed on the altars of the Virgin Mary (the name is a translation of the Spanish for Mary's gold). With the age of exploration, marigold seeds traveled around the world and became a welcome guest just about everywhere. One reason for this plant's popularity is that it is exceptionally easy to grow. It has also served as a plant breeder's dream, and a great variety of improved and enlarged types have been developed. They come in reds, whites, yellows, and shades and combinations in between. They are tall and short, plain and multilayered. Pick whichever suit your sunny garden site best, and water them every weekend.

LILY OF THE VALLEY
(Convallaria majalis)
PERENNIAL

This is a very well-known spring flower. Part of its popularity is due to the ease with which it is grown: Plant it in just about any soil, in sun or shade, and let nature take its course. Another reason for its fame is the dainty, fragrant flowers that it bears: only a quarter of an inch (six millimeters) wide, these appear in the midst of green, eight-inch (twenty-centimeter) leaves. The flowers are lovely in small vase arrangements and are often used in bridal bouquets. Lily of the valley does spread quickly, however; if you have just a small garden, this might not be the plant for you.

MICHAELMAS DAISY, NEW YORK ASTER
(Aster Novi-belgii)
PERENNIAL

This native of the eastern coast of the U.S. is often seen growing wild, a sign that it can thrive without any care at all. Its more refined versions look like junior cousins of the annual garden aster and come in pretty shades of white, pink, and purple. Buy the dwarf varieties; they only grow fifteen inches (thirty-eight centimeters) high and will fill your garden with color in late summer. You will find these are among the easiest of perennials to grow.

PACHYSANDRA, JAPANESE SPURGE
(P. terminalis)
PERENNIAL

If you have a bare, muddy spot under a deep shade tree where it seems nothing will grow, try pachysandra. It has been correctly described as the best ground cover for northern climates. Sometimes called Japanese spurge, this plant remains green year-round and bears small white flowers in the spring. Pachysandra has either all green leaves or ones with white edgings; this last is *P. terminalis* 'Variegata.'

PAINTED DAISY, PYRETHRUM
(Chrysanthemum coccineum)
PERENNIAL

This is a colorful member of the chrysanthemum family that is very easy to grow and that blooms in early summer. Depending on the variety, the plants grow nine inches (twenty-two centimeters) to three feet (ninety centimeters) tall and bear daisylike flowers in shades of white through red. Painted daisies need full sun or very light shade and a weekly watering. No serious pests affect it, and you only have to divide the clumps every four or five years. The foliage is similar to that of wild field daisies and is attractive in the garden after the flowers have stopped blooming.

PANSY
(Viola tricolor hortensis)
PERENNIAL GROWN AS ANNUAL IN COLDER CLIMATES

Poets have sung the praises of these splashy red, yellow, and blue spring flowers since the days of Spenser and Shakespeare. The flowers are a staple of English cottage gardens and have acquired colorful nicknames such as three faces under a hood, herb trinity, love in idleness, and heartsease. Today's garden pansy is a hybrid, a descendent of the wild viola tricolor (often called Johnny-jump-up) and other members of the large viola family. Pansies provide quick and early gratification for the weekend gardener. Buy them at your local nursery in the spring. You will find that there is usually at least one flower blooming on every seedling that you buy; after planting a border or clump, you can stand back and be rewarded with an instant garden. Pansies grow from six inches (fifteen centimeters) to one foot (thirty centimeters) high. If you keep them watered every weekend, pinch their faded flowers, and avoid spots that bake in the sun all day, pansies will bloom well into summer.

PEONY
(Paeonia)
PERENNIAL

This flower has been a garden favorite for centuries. Few plants give such large, beautiful flowers in return for so little effort on the part of the gardener. Give them sun or partial shade, a good rich soil, and a yearly dash of fertilizer, and they will reward you with magnificent pink-and-white late-spring blossoms for thirty years or more. There are thousands of cultivars available. Most have handsome green leaves that grow up to three feet (ninety centimeters) tall and form clumps about three feet (ninety centimeters) wide.

PERIWINKLE, MYRTLE
(Vinca minor)
PERENNIAL

This is an evergreen ground cover that has been popular in American gardens since Colonial times. About the only place where it will not do well is under dry, desertlike conditions. Otherwise, its shiny green leaves will spread throughout the year and be covered with small blue flowers in the spring. Periwinkle likes to take up a lot of room, however; if you have a small garden, it is not for you.

PERENNIAL AGERATUM, MISTFLOWER
(Eupatorium coelestinum)
PERENNIAL

This plant bears blue flowers, which strongly resemble those of the annual ageratum plants, on two-foot (sixty-centimeter) stems in late summer. Its color is a welcome addition at a time when most flowers are red, yellow, or orange. Perennial ageratum is exceptionally easy to grow in sun or partial shade, and it spreads quite rapidly (though this may be a drawback). It needs absolutely no care and is attractive in cut-flower arrangements. If you have room in the garden, set aside a spot or two for this flower.

PETUNIA
ANNUAL

This is the most popular annual in the United States. It likes long, hot summers and lots of sun (a trait inherited from its original Argentine parents). Breeders have found petunias an excellent plant to work with and today there are hundreds of varieties and hybrids. They come in every shade, with flower size ranging from two inches (five centimeters) to seven inches (eighteen centimeters) across. The size of the plants is broken into broad groups, including the dwarf, mound, bedding, giant ruffled, grandiflora, and multiflora doubles. The heights of petunias range from under one foot (thirty centimeters) to almost three feet (ninety centimeters). When planning your summer flower beds, pick a color and a height, and you'll find petunias to match your requirements. They will need water every weekend and a dash of fertilizer about once a month. In return, you will have colorful flowers all summer long.

POT MARIGOLD
(Calendula officinales)
ANNUAL

These flowers have been grown in England for at least four hundred years; Shakespeare referred to them as marygolds. The flowers were once used as medicinal herbs to treat cuts and burns. Today, gardeners find the pot marigold an exceptionally easy plant to grow as long as it has lots of sun and is watered weekly. The flowers look like a cross between a daisy and a chrysanthemum and come in shades of yellow and orange. Depending on the kind of plant, it will grow from ten inches (twenty-five centimeters) to two feet (sixty centimeters) tall. The flowers bloom all summer long and even through a light frost.

SALVIA, SCARLET SAGE
(S. splendens)
ANNUAL

This is an extremely popular red-spiked flower that blooms from early summer until the first frost. It grows slowly throughout the season, starting at about six inches (fifteen centimeters) and reaching up to three feet (ninety centimeters). Salvia is particularly striking in large masses and can often be seen in formal gardens in public parks. Just give it sun or partial shade, a weekly watering, and average soil, and the plant will be set for the summer.

SCILLA
(S. hispanica and *S. siberica)*
PERENNIAL

These are two pretty spring flowers. *S. siberica,* often called Siberian or blue squill, blooms very early and consists of tiny six-inch (fifteen-centimeter-) high blue flowers. *S. hispanica,* or Spanish scilla, is larger (twenty inches, or fifty centimeters, high) and later, blooming toward the end of the daffodil season. This plant has blue or pink flowers and looks like a thin version of a hyacinth. The only work required to have these flowers grow in your garden is to plant their bulbs in the fall. They will bloom and increase in number every year after.

SEDUM, SHOWY STONE CROP
(S. spectabile)
PERENNIAL

This is a plant for a monthly gardener! It has to be one of the toughest in the flower garden; diseases and insects will have nothing to do with it. Every August or thereabouts, it will produce large, flat-headed clusters of small pink flowers on its eighteen-inch (forty-five-centimeter) green, succulent stems. These can be used in cut-flower arrangements or left alone to look pretty in the garden. This is a very neat and tidy plant. It will grow in sun or partial shade and can easily be divided. If you like, put it in a patio pot.

SILVER MOUND, ANGEL'S HAIR, SATINY WORMWOOD
(Artemisia schmidtiana)
PERENNIAL

From a distance, this plant appears to be a beautiful ball of silver cotton candy plunked in the garden. Its feathery, gray foliage contrasts nicely next to the green of spring perennials that are no longer blooming. This plant does not like a lot of water or fertilizer—perfect stipulations for the weekend gardener.

SNOWDROP
(Galanthus nivalis)
PERENNIAL

This is one of the very first flowers to greet spring. Less than one foot (thirty centimeters) tall, it sends forth tiny white flowers that often bloom in the snow. You can plant bulbs just about anywhere in the fall; they will increase on their own and give you pleasure for years to come.

SPIDERWORT
(Tradescantia)
PERENNIAL

This is a North American native that generally likes to grow in a shady spot with moist soil. Up close it can be messy, with its two-foot (sixty-centimeter-) foliage often sprawling about. From afar, however, its blue, pink, or white flowers—opening every morning for almost two summer months—are quite pretty. Recently, hybridizers have crossed two species, *T. bracteata* and *T. virginiana,* and come up with no-care plants bearing names such as blue stone, red cloud, and snow cap; any one or all three would be perfect for a weekend garden.

SUNDROPS
(Oenothera fruticosa)
PERENNIAL

This is a member of the evening primrose family. Some of its close cousins only open their flowers in the evening, but this variety bears gorgeous lemon-yellow flowers during the day in late spring and early summer. The plants grow about two feet (sixty centimeters) tall and bloom for about a month. They are supposed to do best in full sun but will also produce their brilliant colors in partial shade. These plants spread; if they creep out of bounds, they can be easily pulled up because their roots are very shallow. Sundrops are quite tough and will muddle through from year to year without any help from you.

VIRGINIA BLUEBELLS
(Mertensia virginica)
PERENNIAL
These spring flowers send forth one-foot (thirty-centimeter-) to two-foot- (sixty-centimeter-) high stems that appear to have graceful blue bells clinging to their ends. Virginia bluebells are easy to grow if planted in a shady, moist spot and are generally free from pests and diseases. The plant totally disappears by mid-summer, so it is probably best to have these at the back of the garden so their absence will be covered by other flowers in bloom.

SWEET ALYSSUM
(Lobularia maritima)
ANNUAL THAT SELF-SEEDS
This is a terrific plant for the outside border of a garden. It rarely grows more than one foot (thirty centimeters) high (and flops about to look even shorter) and is covered with dainty white flowers, sometimes tinged with purple or pink, from early summer through the first fall frosts. While preferring full sun, it will still grow—though not as well—in partial shade.

YARROW, MILFOIL
(Achillea millefolium 'Fire King')
PERENNIAL
The white-flowered variety of this plant is often seen growing as a weed in open fields. For centuries, its fernlike leaves were used for medicinal purposes in Europe. Though easy to grow, the plant was not a garden favorite because of its floppy, messy tendencies. 'Fire king' is a handsome, modern version. It grows only eighteen inches (forty-five centimeters) tall and will bear flowers for well over a month at the height of summer. Just make sure it has lots of sun, and it will be a nice, comfortable plant for you.

YELLOW ARCHANGEL, SILVER NETTLE
(Lamium galeobdolon)
PERENNIAL
This is another ground cover. The leaves are a pretty silver and green and are particularly suitable for shady spots. In the spring, yellow flowers, somewhat resembling snapdragons, bloom on one-foot- (thirty-centimeter-) high spikes. Spotted dead nettle, *L. maculatum,* is a close cousin of yellow archangel and has pinkish, lavender flowers. Both are exceptionally easy to grow. While some view these plants as weeds, a weekend gardener might find their foliage and flowers an attractive accent in a large, informal setting.

APPENDIX B

PLANTS YOU MIGHT WANT TO TAKE A CHANCE ON

Many of the plants on this list have devoted adherents, who swear that they are exceptionally easy to grow. You will find, however, that other gardeners disagree. In short, these plants do well in some places some of the time but do not thrive in all places all of the time. Others, such as dahlias and roses, might grow well in your garden but do require extra care. The premise of this book is that you will spend no more than two hours a weekend in your garden; you may find you want to increase your garden time to include one of the following.

AFRICAN DAISY
(Arctotis stoechadifolia)
ANNUAL

South African in heritage, this plant likes lots of sun and can go for quite a while without water. If your garden is dry and sunny, this could be a plant for you. Today's hybrids bloom all summer, are only one foot (thirty centimeters) high, and come in pink, red, bronze, yellow, white, and orange.

BELLFLOWER
(Campanula carpatica)
PERENNIAL

A shorter version of Canterbury bell, this plant adds a nice splash of blue or white color to the summer border. In the past decade, British breeders have developed several handsome dwarf—about one foot (thirty centimeters) tall—plants with names such as wedgewood, white star, and white carpet. Look for these if you decide to include bellflowers in your garden. The plants are susceptible to a disease called crown rot, so make sure they are not in continually damp soil. They do not like drought either, so you will have to water them weekly.

DAHLIA
ANNUAL

These elegant, aristocratic flowers come in nearly every color except blue. They were discovered in Mexico and Guatemala by Spanish explorers in the 16th century. It took almost two hundred years before specimens were sent across the ocean to the Madrid Botanic Garden. There, the plant was named in honor of the great Swedish botanist, Andre Dahl. The plant became very popular, and today there are over one thousand varieties; most bloom during the latter part of summer. Dahlias suffer during prolonged periods of dry, hot weather; often require extensive spraying to ward off insects and diseases; must be watered continuously; and usually require staking—all drawbacks for the weekend gardener.

ENGLISH PRIMROSE
(Primula vulgaris)
PERENNIAL

This is a wonderful addition to a spring garden, one clump can produce over one hundred flowers on six-inch (fifteen-centimeter) to nine-inch (twenty-two-centimeter) stems. Thanks to the development of hybrids, primroses come in a wide range of colors, such as orange, purple, and yellow. Primroses like humid climates and do not do well in afternoon sun.

FORGET-ME-NOT
(Myosotis sylvatica)
ANNUAL

There are several plants that are called forget-me-not. This particular one thrives in cool, moist soil; grows no taller than one foot (thirty centimeters); and bears dainty blue flowers in the spring. The plants are easy to start: Just throw seeds about your bulb beds in the fall, and the plants will reseed themselves every year after that. Forget-me-not looks best in large spreads. This could be a drawback for a weekend gardener who may not be able to give them the space they deserve.

FOUR O'CLOCK, MARVEL OF PERU, BEAUTY OF THE NIGHT
(Mirabilis jalapa)
ANNUAL

These two-foot- (sixty-centimeter-) to three-foot- (ninety-centimeter-) high plants have small white, yellow, red, or pink trumpet-shaped blossoms that supposedly open at four o'clock in the afternoon; hence, the popular name. They are native to Central America and Peru (hence another popular name) and are grown as perennials in warmer climates. Self-seeding quite readily, four o'clocks sometimes appear to be a perennial in colder places. Four o'clocks will add nothing very special to your garden, but they are easy to grow (just water weekly) and might be perfect for some weekend gardens.

GAILLARDIA, BLANKET FLOWER
(G. aristata)
PERENNIAL

These flowers resemble black-eyed Susans, except they have red rather than black centers. Many hybrids have been developed, and there are now annual plants to choose from (*G. pulchella* is quite nice). All grow two feet (sixty centimeters) to three feet (ninety centimeters) tall and bloom all summer through early frosts. The seed heads, however, are rather unattractive, and the plants tend to sprawl. If you don't mind a messy spot of color, this could be the plant for you.

GEUM
(G. chiloense 'Mrs. John Bradshaw')
PERENNIAL

This plant has low, attractive green foliage throughout the year and sends forth a profusion of red, yellow, or orange flowers on two-foot (sixty-centimeter) stems from May to August. If you plant geum in the right place, you will have a delightful garden friend that requires little attention except for weekly watering during drought. If they aren't put in a sunny location with excellent drainage, however, these plants often refuse to grow.

IVY
(Hedera)
PERENNIAL

The English gardener Gertrude Jekyll wrote that the word "ivy" was among the oldest in the English language, being pure Anglo-Saxon and coming down through history unaltered in sound. *H. helix*, English ivy, has long been special to those living in Great Britain and was one of the first plants brought to the New World by colonists. Today, there are over fifty species of just this one variety. Ivy is so well-known as a ground cover that it needs no description. While it is easy to cultivate and spreads readily, it is not hardy in colder climates.

LAVENDER, ENGLISH LAVENDER
(*Lavandula angustifolia*)
PERENNIAL

This herb has been grown for centuries for its aromatic oil and is named for the color of its flowers, which bloom for almost two full summer months. Lavender grows in bushy clumps, about two feet (sixty centimeters) wide, that remain gray-green throughout the season. The plants must be trimmed every spring; even so, they still get leggy and unattractive after three or four years and need to be replanted. Lavender generally grows about two feet (sixty centimeters) tall, but new dwarf varieties are only one foot (thirty centimeters) tall and might be more suited to the weekend garden.

LILY
(*Lilium*)
PERENNIAL

"Lilies [are] some of the most stately and beautiful of garden flowers," Gertrude Jekyll wrote almost a century ago. With their tall stems crowned with elegant, trumpet-shaped flowers, lilies add regal splendor to any setting. Vigorous breeding programs have added hundreds of new varieties and hybrids to the plants already in existence. There are tough ones—the tiger lily grows wild in the U.S.—and tender ones nurtured by dedicated horticulturalists. There are tall—twelve foot (three and a half meters)—and short—one foot (thirty centimeters)—lilies, ones that blossom in late spring and ones that bloom in early fall. The flowers come in an amazing range of shapes and colors. Most, however, take some work to ensure that they are planted in the right place and that they do not succumb to various diseases. If you want this lovely plant in your garden, talk to your local nursery to see what is best for your area and your garden.

NASTURTIUM
(*Tropaeolum*)
ANNUAL

These flowers hail from the Andes mountains and like a cool spot in which to grow. They start blooming in early summer and keep right on going until knocked down by frost. Avoid the trailing nasturtiums; the bush kind grow only one foot (thirty centimeters) high and are covered with pretty orange, yellow, red, or purple flowers that are quite nice in arrangements. Nasturtiums have an unfortunate quality of attracting hoards of black aphids; if this happens in your garden, it is best to pull up the plants and just throw them away.

NICOTIANA, FLOWERING TOBACCO
(N. alata)
ANNUAL

A cousin of the plant whose leaves are used for cigarettes and cigars, this plant used to be known for its lovely scent, which would waft across lawns on warm summer evenings. That plant, however, is tall and leggy, and shorter hybrids have been developed. These come in a range of colors from white through pink to purple. Unfortunately, these newer versions do not have the exquisite aroma of their weedier ancestor. In addition, both kinds of nicotiana tend to attract pests; although they are able to resist them, nearby plants often succumb.

ORIENTAL POPPY
(Papaver orientale)
PERENNIAL

This is a striking, handsome flower, but because its bloom period at the beginning of summer is short, it may not be ideally suited for the weekend garden. There are over sixty different plants available, in pink, white, red, orange, and yellow colors. The flower size varies from four inches (ten centimeters) to ten inches (twenty-five centimeters). The taller four-foot (120-centimeter) plants should be avoided because they generally need stak-

ing; cultivars between two feet (sixty centimeters) and three feet (ninety centimeters) should not present this problem. The foliage of the plant disappears by mid-summer and then reappears in the fall, leaving a bare spot in your garden in the between period.

THE PEARL, SNEEZEWORT
(Achillea ptarmica)
PERENNIAL

This is an old-fashioned garden favorite. It got its second name, sneezewort, because its roots were dried and used as snuff in Colonial times. This plant features clusters of small white flowers with yellow

centers. The bloom period is from June to September, a definite plus for the weekender. While less than three feet (ninety centimeters) tall, the pearl does have a tendency to flop and look messy in the garden.

PERSIAN BUTTERCUP
(Ranunculus asiaticus)
PERENNIAL TREATED AS ANNUAL IN COLDER CLIMATES

These bright red, yellow, white, and pink flowers resemble small peonies. They grow about one and a half feet (forty-five centimeters) tall and add spectacular springtime color to gardens all along the California coast, where they are treated as a perennial. In colder climates, the tender tubers can be planted in spring for summer bloom in a partially shaded area. These tubers must be dug up in the fall if they are to bloom again the next year.

PHLOX
(Polimoniaceae)
PERENNIAL

These are tall—three feet (ninety centimeters) to four feet (120 centimeters)— plants that bear large clumps of pink, purple, or white flowers at their tips. They look lovely at the rear of a summer garden. Unfortunately, frequent attacks by pests such as red spider mites and diseases such as powdery mildew reduce the value of this plant. The late British army captain B. Symons-Jeune, one of the most famous breeders of phlox, developed a new strain that is more resistant to fungus, has a long bloom period, and is generally strong enough not to be staked. If you decide you want summer phlox in your garden, be sure it is a Symons-Jeune plant.

PINCUSHION FLOWER
(Scabiosa caucasica)
PERENNIAL

The Latin, botanical, name for this plant derived because it is thought to cure scabies, an itch. The popular name comes from its appearance: The stamens in the center rise one inch above the rest of the flower and look like pins stuck in a cush-

ion. If planted in the right location, this two-foot- (sixty-centimeter-) tall plant adds a delicate touch of blue to a summer garden. The problem, once again, is finding the perfect spot for it. The plant can be killed by summer drought or by excessive winter or spring rains. On the plus side, it can bloom from June through September and is excellent in cut-flower arrangements.

PORTULACA
(P. grandiflora)
ANNUAL

If you have a sunny, dry, preferably sandy spot, this is a perfect plant for the border of a weekend garden. Growing only eight inches (twenty centimeters) high, portulaca will bear bright white, pink, yellow, red, and purple flowers throughout the summer. It is sometimes called rose moss because the flowers resemble small roses. These flowers close at night and then open up to greet the sun each morning. They will not survive in hazy, cloudy climates.

ROSE
(Rosaceae)
PERENNIAL

A rose by any name represents work in a garden, and a great deal of loveliness as well. Historical records indicate that the rose was the first cultivated flower. The

Greeks, during the height of their civilization, called it "the queen of flowers," and many agree with that description today. If you have your heart set on roses, choose a species rather than a hybrid plant. Check with your local nursery to review ones that are hardy to your area and that are least prone to diseases and pests.

SHASTA DAISY
(Chrysanthemum x superbum)
PERENNIAL

This is the hybrid member of the chrysanthemum family that produces the white daisies most often seen in floral bouquets from shops. If not attacked by pests or diseases, this can be a wonderful plant in the garden. It grows two feet (sixty centimeters) to four feet (120 centimeters) tall and will bear flowers all summer through frosts. Since the shasta daisy is so susceptible to various illnesses, however, a weekend gardener is taking a risk in trying to grow it.

SNAPDRAGONS
(Antirrhinum majus)
ANNUAL

These are such pretty plants—adding spikes of red, purple, pink, white, or yellow to the summer garden—that it is hard to resist them. However, a weekend gardener should only grow the shorter vari-

eties and should know that the plants do need to have the spent blossoms removed every weekend (otherwise bloom ceases) and that diseases often strike.

SNOW ON THE MOUNTAIN, GOUTWEED
(Aegopodium podagraria)
PERENNIAL

This is viewed as an unmitigated pest in some places and as a fantastic ground cover in others. It spreads fast and smothers everything in its path. In compensation, however, it has attractive green-and-white leaves and bears airy white flowers on twelve-inch (thirty-centimeter) stems in early summer. This plant will grow wherever it is planted: in poor or rich soil, in dry or wet spots, in sun or shade.

SPEEDWELL
(Veronica longifolia)
PERENNIAL

Growing up to two and a half feet (seventy-six centimeters) tall, the long, blue spikes of this plant are a nice addition to the garden in July and August—if they are staked. While preferring full sun, this plant will also tolerate partial shade. It is subject to several diseases and should be divided every four years—two more factors that might deter its appearance in the weekend garden.

STRAWFLOWER
(Helichrysum bracteatum)
ANNUAL

These pretty flowers are also known as everlastings in recognition of the ease in which they can be dried. The tall varieties reach three feet (ninety centimeters) and tend to flop dreadfully. The weekend gardener had best look for the shorter hybrids, which come in happy summer colors such as white, orange, red, and yellow, and which will bloom to frost. When given full sun and long, hot summers, strawflowers are a wonderful addition to the garden. A Victorian favorite, many glass paperweights from that era still bear testimony to their bright colors and everlasting qualities.

SWEET WILLIAM
(Dianthus barbatus)
ANNUAL, BIENNIAL, OR PERENNIAL, DEPENDING ON LOCATION AND STRAIN

This is a low-growing, old-fashioned garden favorite. In early- and midsummer it bears fistfuls of flowers in shades of white through red. While very pretty in bloom, the plant is rather nondescript once the flowers are gone.

TREASURE FLOWER
(Gazania)
ANNUAL

Another South African native, treasure flower does well in hot, dry weather and likes lots of sun and sandy well-drained soil. Given those conditions, its daisylike blooms in red, pink, yellow, orange, and bronze colors are a beautiful addition to the garden. The plants grow six inches (fifteen centimeters) to fifteen inches (thirty-eight centimeters) high; many sprawl attractively. Treasure flower thrives on the California coast and can be seen in large groupings along the highways.

TULIPS
PERENNIAL

It is hard to comprehend today, but these tall, elegant spring flowers were the cause of one of the greatest financial crashes in history. The flowers were discovered growing in Turkey by the Spanish ambassador in 1554. He brought several bulbs back to Europe, where they gradually piqued the interest of horticulturalists. The Dutch, enjoying a period of great prosperity, began to bid up the price of bulbs as part of a fashionable garden. Someone decided there was money in the demand for bulbs. Soon, a lot of people decided they couldn't lose with bulbs. Between 1634 and 1637, speculative hysteria affected Holland. At one time, tulip bulbs were actually more valuable than their equivalent weight in gold. As with all financial crazes, this one eventually ended, but the Dutch economy was weak for more than a century as a result. The Dutch, however, never lost their attraction for the tulip and remain its major exporters. Hundreds of varieties and hybrids are available in all colors and sizes. Tulips, however, present some problems for a weekend gardener. Many do not have long bloom periods, lose all bloom after two or three years, and have unattractive foliage after the flowers are gone. If you have a small garden, tulips are probably not for you. If you have a large one or a spot that you are not particularly fussy about, include tulips by all means.

WISHBONE FLOWER
(Torenia fournieri)
ANNUAL

This has been described as a little gem. It's very easy to grow, gets about twelve inches (thirty centimeters) high, and bears lots of flowers that look somewhat like snapdragons in size and shape but have pansy colors. This plant likes lots of shade and water. If you can find a spot that meets these requirements, you might try wishbone flowers in your garden.

ZINNIA
(Zinnia elegans)
ANNUAL

This is another popular summer flower. Native to Mexico, zinnias have now been developed by breeders to come in every color except blue and green and to range in height from dwarf to tall. Weekend gardeners should avoid the latter because they must be staked. The plants continue to develop new flower blossoms all summer long and, when in bloom, the flowers last quite long and are excellent in cut-flower arrangements. These plants must have full sun, and faded flowers should be snipped. Zinnias tend to get mildew, a major drawback for a weekend gardener. If you want to try them anyway, give them lots of air and water only the roots and not the foliage; these measures should help deter disease.

APPENDIX C

PLANTS YOU SHOULD PROBABLY AVOID

The plants listed below are among those that just are not suitable for a weekend gardener with limited amounts of time. These plants have a variety of drawbacks: too tall, too fussy about location, too tender, or too prone to diseases such as mildew and root rot. Admittedly, many of these plants are lovely. Once you have gotten the hang of being a weekend gardener, you might want to take on the challenge of growing some of them.

ASTER
(Callistephus chinensis)

BABY'S BREATH
(Gypsophila elegans)

BACHELOR'S BUTTON
(Centaurea cyanus)

BLACK SNAKEROOT
(Cimicifuga racemosa)

CALADIUM

CALLA

CANNA

CANTERBURY BELL
(Campanula medium)

CARNATION
(Dianthus caryophyllus)

CARDINAL FLOWER
(Lobelia cardinalis)

CLEMATIS

COSMOS

DELPHINIUM

FOXGLOVE
(Digitalis)

GLADIOLUS

**GOLDEN MARGUERITE,
KELWAYI YELLOW**
(Anthemis tinctoria)

HELIOPSIS

HIBISCUS

HOLLYHOCK
(Alcea rosea)

LAMB'S EAR
(Stachys byzantine)

LEOPARD'S BANE
(Doronicum cordatum)

LUPINE

MALTESE CROSS
(Lychnis Chalcedonica)

MEXICAN SUNFLOWER
(Tithonia)

PAINTED TONGUE
(Salpiglossis sinuata)

PENSTEMON

PURPLE CONEFLOWER
(Echinacea purpurea)

RED HOT POKER
(Kniphofia uvaria)

ROSE MALLOW
(Hibiscus moscheutos)

SPIDER PLANT
(Cleome)

STOCKS
(Matthiola incana)

STOKES' ASTER
(Stokesia laevis)

SUNFLOWER
(Helianthus)

SWAN RIVER DAISY
(Brachycome iberidifolia)

TRANSVAAL DAISY
(Gerbera)

VERBENA

WALLFLOWER
(Cheiranthus cheiri)

WINDFLOWER
(Anemone)

APPENDIX D

SOURCES

The following nurseries comprise the membership of the Mail Order Association of Nurserymen. The ninety-four firms on the list are located in both the United States and Canada. All offer catalogues that may be ordered by simply writing to the firm at the address below. Unless otherwise indicated, the catalogues are free of charge.

As a help to consumers, the Association offers the following guidelines when buying plants through the mail:

■ Don't be misled by fantastic claims such as promises of miracle growth or yields, or unbelievably low prices.

■ Read catalogue descriptions carefully before buying to be sure you are ordering what you really want and can grow in your climate.

■ Fill out the order blank clearly and completely. Don't forget to include your complete street address for UPS deliveries, zip code, and, if requested, tax and shipping charges.

■ If you do not want a substitute in the event that the item you order is sold out, state so clearly.

■ If you require a specific delivery date, state so clearly.

■ Keep a record or a copy of your order.

■ Never send cash through the mail.

■ Check and understand the company's guarantee policy.

■ When the order is delivered, make sure it is complete.

■ Plant your new purchases as soon as possible. If something fails to grow, notify the nursery immediately.

ABBEY GARDENS
Dept. MN
4620 Carpenteria Avenue
Carpenteria, CA 93013

VERNON BARNES & SON
P.O. Box 250LMN
McMinnville, TN 37110

BEATITUDE WREATH
P.O. Box 14MN
South Gouldsboro, ME 04678

BEERSHEBA WILDFLOWER GARDEN
P.O. Box 551
Stone Door MN
Beersheba Springs, TN 37305

BLUESTONE PERENNIALS
Dept. 47
7211 Middle Ridge Road
Madison, OH 44057

BOUNTIFUL RIDGE
Dept. MN
P.O. Box 250
Princess Anne, MD 21853

BRECK'S
Dept. MN
6523 North Galena Road
Peoria, IL 61632

BROOKFIELD NURSERY & TREE PLANTATION
P.O. Box 151MN
844 Hutcheson Drive
Blacksburg, VA 24060

BUNTING'S NURSERIES, INC.
Dept. MN
Duke's Street,
P.O. Box 306
Selbyville, DE 19975

BURGESS SEED & PLANT CO.
Dept. 39-50
905 Four Seasons Road
Bloomington, IL 61701

W. ATLEE BURPEE SEED CO.
Dept. MN
Burpee Building, No. 12
Warminster, PA 18974

BY HAND AND FOOT LTD
P.O. Box 611MN
Brattleboro, VT 05301

CALIFORNIA EPI CENTER
Dept. MN
Box 1431
Vista, CA 92083
Catalog Price: $1.00

CALIFORNIA NURSERY CO.
P.O. Box 2278MN
Fremont, CA 94536

CAPABILITY'S BOOKS FOR GARDENERS
Box 114
Dept. MN
Highway 46
Deer Park, WI 54007

THE CLAPPER CO.
Box A
Dept. MN
West Newton, MA 02165

CLIFFORD'S PERENNIAL & VINE
Route 2
Box 320MN
East Troy, WI 53120

DAVIDSON WILSON GREENHOUSES
Route 2
Dept. MN
Crawfordsville, IN 47933

DAYSTAR
RFD No. 2
Box 250MN
Litchfield, ME 04350

DEJAGER BULBS
Dept. MAN
188 Asbury Street
South Hamilton, MA 01982

DUTCH GARDENS, INC.
Dept. MN
P.O. Box 168
Montvale, NJ 07645

DUTCH MOUNTAIN NURSERY
Dept. MAN
7984 North 48th Street, R-1
Augusta, MI 49012

EMLONG NURSERIES, INC.
Dept. MN
2671 West Marquette Woods Road
Stevensville, MI 49127

FARMER SEED & NURSERY
Dept. MN
818 NW 4th Street
Faribault, MN 55021

FERRIS NURSERY & GARDEN CENTER
Dept. 801
811 4th Street NE
Hampton, IA 50441

HENRY FIELD SEED & NURSERY CO.
Dept. MN
407 Sycamore Street
Shenandoah, IA 51602

FLEMING'S FLOWER FIELDS
Dept. MAN
P.O. Box 4607
Lincoln, NE 68504

DEAN FOSTER NURSERIES
Dept. MAN
R. NO. 2
Hartford, MI 49057

GATEWAY SEED CO.
101 5th Avenue
P.O. Box 906MN
Clinton, IA 52732

GLORIA DEI MINIATURE ROSES
36 East Road, Dept. MN
High Falls, NY 12440

GRACE'S GARDENS
MN Bay Street
Westport, CT 06880

GREEN TECH NURSERY
53 Four Mile Road South
Dept. MN
Traverse City, MI 49684

GREENLIFE GARDENS GREENHOUSES
Dept. MN
101 County Line Road
Griffin, GA 30223

GURNEY SEED & NURSERY
Dept. MN
Gurney Building
Yankton, SD 57078

HANA GARDENLAND
P.O. Box 248 MAN
Hana, Hawaii 96713

HARRIS SEEDS
3670 Buffalo Road
Dept. MN
Rochester, NY 14624

H. G. HASTINGS
P.O. Box 4274
Dept. M
Atlanta, GA 30302

HERBST BROTHERS
SEEDSMEN
Dept. MN
1000 North Main Street
Brewster, NY 10509

HOLBROOK FARM AND
NURSERY
Route 2
Box 223B MN
Fletcher, NC 28732

HOUSE OF WESLEY
Dept. MN
2200 East Oakland Avenue
Bloomington, IL 61701

HOUSTON DAYLILY
GARDENS, INC.
P.O. Box 7008
Dept. MN
The Woodlands, TX 77380

INTER-STATE NURSERIES,
INC.
Dept. MN
504 E Street
Hamburg, IA 51640

JACKSON & PERKINS
Dept. MAN
P.O. Box 1028
Medford, OR 97501

J. W. JUNG SEED CO.
Dept. MN
Box 385
Randolph, WE 53956

KELLY BROTHERS
NURSERIES, INC.
Dept. MN
Maple Street
Dansville, NY 14437

KRIDER NURSERIES, INC.
Dept. MAN
P.O. Box 29
Middlebury, IN 46540

LAKELAND NURSERIES
SALES
Dept. MN
Unique Merchandise Mart
Bldg. NR 4
Hanover, PA 17333

OROL LEDDEN & SONS
P.O. Box 7
Dept. MN
Sewell, NJ 08080

HENRY LEUTHARDT
NURSERIES, INC.
Dept. MN
Montauk Highway
East Moriches, NY 11940

LEWIS STRAWBERRY
NURSERY, INC.
Dept. MN
P.O. Box 24
Rocky Point, NC 28457

LOCKHART SEEDS
P.O. Box 1361 MN
3 North Wilson Way
Stockton, CA 95201

LOUISIANA NURSERY
Route 7
Box 43 MN
Opelousas, LA 70570

MAKIELSKI BERRY FARM
& NURSERY
7130 Platt MN
Ypsilanti, MI 48197

EARL MAY SEED &
NURSERY CO.
Dept. MN
208 North Elm Street
Shenandoah, IA 51603

McCONNELL NURSERIES,
INC.
Dept. MAN
Port Burwell, Ontario
Canada NOJ ITO

MELLINGERS NURSERY,
INC.
Dept. 2342
West South Range Road
North Lima, OH 44452

MICHIGAN BULB CO.
Dept. MN
1950 Waldorf NW
Grand Rapids, MI 49550

J. E. MILLER NURSERIES,
INC.
Dept. MN
5061 West Lake Road
Canandaigua, NY 14424

THE MINI FARM
Turnbull Rd., Route 1
Box 501M
Bonaqua, TN 37025

MUSSER FORESTS, INC.
Dept. MN
P.O. Box 340
Indiana, PA 15701

NOR'EAST MINIATURE ROSES
58 Hammond Street MN
Rowley, MA 01969

L. L. OLDS SEED CO.
Box 7790 MN
Madison, WI 53707

GEORGE W. PARK SEED CO.
Dept. MN
P.O. 32
Greenwood, SC 29640

PIEDMONT PLANT CO.
P.O. Box 424 B
Albany, GA 31703

PROTEA GARDENS OF MAUI
R.R. 2
Box 389 MAN
Kula, Maui, Hawaii 96790

PUTNEY NURSERY, INC.
Box MO
Putney, VT 05346

QUALITY DUTCH BULBS
50 Lake Drive
Dept. MN, P.O. Box 225
Hillsdale, NJ 07642

RAINBOW GARDENS NURSERY & BOOKSHOP
P.O. Box 721, Dept. MAN
La Habra, CA 90631

RAYNER BROS., INC.
P.O. Box 1617—MAN
Salisbury, MD 21801

RHAPIS GARDENS
P.O. Drawer 287M
Gregory, TX 78359

RIVERLAND GARDENS
2700 Brabant Marineau
St. Laurent, Quebec
Canada H4S IT7

ROSEHILL FARM
Box 406
Gregg Neck Rd. MN
Galena, MD 21635

SHADY HILL GARDENS
821M Walnut Street
Batavia, IL 60510

SINGER'S GROWING THINGS
17806 Plummer Street
Dept. M
Northridge, CA 91325

SMITH & HAWKEN
68 M Homer
Palo Alto, CA 94301

SOUTHMEADOW FRUIT GARDENS
Box GM
Lakeside, MI 49116

SPRING HILL NURSERIES
Dept. MN
6523 North Galena Road
Peoria, IL 61601

SPRUCE BROOK NURSERY
Route 118
Dept. MAN
Litchfield, CT 06759

STARK BRO'S NURSERIES
Box B2968A
Louisiana, MO 63353

STERN'S NURSERIES, INC.
Dept. M
607 West Washington Street
Geneva, NY 14456

SUNNYBROOK FARMS NURSERY
P.O. Box 6 MN
9448 Mayfield Road
Chesterland, OH 44026

SUNSWEET NURSERY
Box D
Dept. MAN
Sumner, GA 31789

SWAN ISLAND DAHLIAS
P.O. Box 800 MN
Canby, OR 97013

TAYLOR'S HERB GARDEN
1535 Lone Oak Road
Dept. MN
Vista, CA 92083

VAN BOURGONDIEN BROS.
Dept. MN
245 Route 109
P.O. Box A
Babylon, NY 11702

VAN NESS WATER GARDENS
Dept. MAN
2460 North Euclid Avenue
Upland, CA 91786

VANS PINES
7550 144th Avenue, Dept. MN
West Olive, MI 49460

VERMONT BEAN SEED CO.
Garden Lane
Box 308MN
Bomoseen, VT 05732

WAYNESBORO NURSERIES, INC.
P.O. Box 987 MAN
Waynesboro, VA 22980

THE WAYSIDE GARDENS CO.
Dept. WG
Hodges, SC 29695

WHITE FLOWER FARM
Dept. MN
Litchfield, CT 06759

WINTERTHUR PLANT SHOP
Winterthur Museum
Dept. MA
Winterthur, DE 19735

WOLFE NURSERY
Dept. MN
500 Terminal Road
Fort Worth, TX 76106

INDEX

Front cover photograph by **Derek Fell**

PICTURE CREDITS

ABOUT THE AUTHOR

PATRICIA A. TAYLOR, a freelance writer and editor, has been a gardener from the age of six on. She has written articles on a wide variety of topics for numerous publications, including The New York Times, Self, Working Woman, Cosmopolitan, Family Circle, and Organic Gardening. Taylor lives and gardens in Princeton, New Jersey.